FROM BANGKOK TO SIBERIA VIA THE MARRAKECH EXPRESS

By the same author:

Footsteps of the Celts by Rail, Book Guild Publishing 2009

Rails Over the Andes, Athena Press 2007

FROM BANGKOK TO SIBERIA VIA THE MARRAKECH EXPRESS

William Bleasdale

Book Guild Publishing
Sussex, England

First published in Great Britain in 2011 by
The Book Guild Ltd
Pavilion View
19 New Road
Brighton, BN1 1UF

Typesetting in Garamond by
Keyboard Services, Luton, Bedfordshire

Printed and bound in Spain under the supervision of
MRM Graphics Ltd, Winslow, Bucks

A catalogue record for this book is available from
The British Library.

ISBN 978 1 84624 624 1

To Annie
with love

Contents

Acknowledgements

The black and white photographs of the Thailand–Burma Railway are reproduced by kind permission of the Thailand–Burma Railway Centre, Kanchanaburi, Thailand.

The map of Circum–Baikal Railway is reproduced courtesy of www.waytorussia.net travel guide.

The photograph of Ipoh Railway Station is reproduced courtesy of Roszaimy Yaacob.

PART I

Thailand and Malaysia

Following my trips to South America, North Africa and the British Isles, this is my first venture onto the railways of Asia and I have been looking forward to it with great anticipation. The journey will take me some 500 miles from Chiang Mai in the north of Thailand to the capital, Bangkok; from there, there will be excursions to the Grand Palace, The Rose Garden and Culture Centre followed by a journey to Kanchanaburi for a ride on the Burma Death Railway to Wang Pho. I will then be taking the overnight train from Bangkok, through Malaysia, to Kuala Lumpur where I will spend about three days.

After a short flight from Manchester I arrive at Heathrow Terminal 5, not without some trepidation after all the horror stories about lost luggage and delayed flights. In the end the reality is quite different, but it is a surprise that it is a twenty-five minute bus drive to transfer to Terminal 4, that vast shopping centre and airport terminal.

The flight to Bangkok is twelve hours overnight but I find that I have the luxury of three empty seats alongside me and I am able to stretch out and get a reasonable night.

Bangkok airport terminal is new and is a vast high domed place of steel, concrete and glass. It is also on many levels and when I eventually arrive at the departure gate for local fights to Chiang Mai the bad news is that there is a four-hour wait. This means that when I eventually arrive the journey will have taken me twenty-one hours from Manchester.

The local currency is the Thai baht at about 62 to the pound and it takes a little while to appreciate that an extremely good and large cup of coffee is not actually expensive at 25 baht.

It is time to head for the departure gate and here I find that security is very tight; they won't even allow me to take a small 100ml bottle of water through. Following me is a Buddhist monk in his flowing browny-orange robe, and he is not only subjected to the personal body scan but is searched as well during which his bare stomach is exposed. I find the whole episode embarrassing. Goodness knows what he thought.

Sitting in my seat on the Boeing 747 to Chiang Mai, waiting for take off, I idly study the flight plan, which tells me that it is 370 miles to Chiang Mai and that the temperature outside is 86F; it also shows that our altitude is varying from 46 to 49 feet. I'm not sure how that is possible while sitting on the ground.

Chiang Mai airport is quite a contrast, being very clean and bright with no steel or concrete in sight. There are beautiful polished floors. Baggage claim and immigration are very efficient and I am very soon on my way to the exit door but as I walk through, it is like walking into a wall of heat. Chiang Mai, often called the Rose of the North, is Thailand's second most important city and was originally chosen by King Mengrai in 1292 as the capital of his Lanna kingdom which at that time included all of the northern 'bulge' of Thailand and part of southern Burma. Wars became commonplace and eventually the Burmese took back the Lanna capital in 1615 but were later defeated by allied Lanna and Siamese forces and from then on Lanna remained an autonomous region until the nineteenth century.

Home for the next three nights is a very nice hotel on Chang Klan Road in the commercial part of the city, just fifteen minutes from the airport and midway between the railway station and the original walled city. Although the walls of the ancient city were largely destroyed in the Second World War the vestiges of those sections that remain are in good condition. Looking at my map I can see that the moat that surrounded the walled city is, surprisingly, still intact and in many places I can see that it is also tree-lined.

Part of the original city wall

I have been looking forward to eating in Thailand as at home I enjoy both cooking and eating Thai meals. Tonight there is only time for dinner and bed as there is an early start tomorrow. The dining room is very attractive with bamboo furniture and heavy green tiled floors and on entering I learn my first Thai word, which is *Sawasdee* (the second s is silent) meaning hello or a general greeting. At the door a traditionally dressed young girl greets me with that word and the *wai*. The *wai* is the Thai greeting and involves the palms being pressed together and lifted towards the chin. There are complexities with the *wai* regarding class, age and gender but western visitors are not seriously expected to know or observe them.

Now for the business of eating, and there is a serious amount of choice with starters, main course and sweets. Sweets seems a very appropriate term as there are some extremely dainty and delicious-looking offerings, which seem mainly to involve cream, jelly, chocolate and fruit on top of little squares of sponge cake that are filled with some sort of butter cream. In the end I settle for two main courses starting with battered fish in a sweet and sour sauce followed by a beef mussaman curry which starts by being quite mild but gets hotter as it goes on. Both dishes are quite delicious.

There is live entertainment at dinner by a trio dressed in outlandishly bright shirts. Their choice of music is interesting, although I did not particularly take note of what they were singing I do remember Cliff Richard's *Lovin' Doll* and *Smoke gets in your eyes* by the Platters.

After a good night in a very luxurious bedroom I am up at 6 am. Outside it is very misty with the mountains vaguely outlined in the background. I have now just about got my head round what day it is after all that travelling, and the fact that it is today here and yesterday at home.

Today, there is a visit to one of the most revered Buddhist shrines in northern Thailand which, to give it its full title, is Wat Phrathat Doi Suthep Ravvoravihara. But first is breakfast and I choose fried noodles with egg, bacon and sea bass, preceded by fresh pineapple. I could really get used to this way of eating.

Driving through the town I notice the dusty side streets festooned with telephone and electric cables are faintly reminiscent of some South American towns. In the suburbs there are lots of mimosa and forsythia trees and bushes of bright red hibiscus. The shrine is situated on the top of a forest-covered mountain high above the city, and as we leave the houses and head west the road winds steeply up the hillside; sometimes the coach is reduced to grinding upwards in bottom gear.

On the way I notice some electricity pylons with plastic sleeves halfway up and when I ask what they are for I learn that the sleeves are to prevent rats climbing to the top of the pylon and chewing the cables. It seemed an unlikely explanation but who can say. There are a lot of banana trees and suddenly the road widens out to reveal lots of souvenir stalls and restaurants. We have arrived.

Wat Phrathat Doi Suthep Ravvoravihara was founded in the fourteenth century and many people regard it as a symbol of Lanna Thailand. It also contains a lot of sacred relics.

To get to the temple you can either climb the 306 steps of the Naga stairs or ride a modern funicular railway; it is too hot for 306 steps but there are many people going that way, including a lot of young Buddhist monks. At the top there is an interesting tree that at first sight I thought was a coconut palm but when I ask I learn that it is the cannon ball tree, and looking at the large brown fruits hanging from it I can see that it is very aptly named.

The cannon ball tree

After taking off my shoes I enter the courtyard by some steps and in front of me is the main *wihan*, which is 500 years old. Inside is a huge Buddha surrounded by several smaller ones and these figures are the most important within the temple complex.

The centrepiece of the shrine is the Stup Pagoda (Golden Chedi) and it sits in a courtyard surrounded by various buildings. It is 79 feet high

The main *wihan*

and 39 feet across at the base and its covering of engraved gold plate is positively dazzling in the bright sunshine; it is surrounded by four ornamental umbrellas which are brightly gilded and covered with very attractive filigree decorations.

Golden Chedi

There are a lot of people about including many young people who have come with flowers to offer and to pray and prostrate themselves, oblivious of the surge of people around them. Thailand is 96% Buddhist and the people take their religion seriously. They believe in perpetual reincarnation where each life is influenced by their actions in the previous one and this philosophy is known as *karma. Nirvana*, or enlightenment, is the only state that will end the cycle of rebirth, and to attain *nirvana* Buddhists must develop meditation, morality and wisdom. In the short time that I have been here I have seen what a friendly people they are. Not for nothing is it known as the land of smiles where most people practise tolerance and non-violence.

The courtyard and buildings are surrounded by a wide walkway and here there is an almost constant chiming of bells, coming from a row of temple bells suspended on a bar which used to be for calling monks to worship but now seem to be for visitors to ring for good luck. The interior walls of the courtyard are covered with drawings depicting the life of Buddha and there are also many effigies.

The temple bells

A Buddha image

At the far end there is a view point from which you get a panoramic view of Chiang Mai five thousand feet below. Today is not a good day to see the city as there is a lot of haze which is not just caused by the heat but is also due to smoke resulting from the slash and burn policy of some hill tribes who clear trees for farmland. This in turn creates flooding problems for Chiang Mai because tree clearance means that when the rains come the ground cannot hold the water and the city suffers floods quite often.

A few yards away is the temple museum guarded by two splendid *naga* figures. *Nagas* are mythical serpents and fulfil a protective role in keeping away bad spirits and they can be seen throughout Thailand. A

The temple museum

few yards away there is a short flight of steps flanked by palms with a Buddha sculpture at the top.

This has been a very interesting and enjoyable visit and the position of the temple on top of a mountain with trees on all sides falling away down the mountainside and forming part of the Doi Suthep-Doi Pui National Park make it a very pleasant place to be. I decide that I must use the steps to go down. They are beautifully paved with side walls formed as part of the body of *naga* figures and going down I can only admire the stamina of those that are climbing upwards in this heat as even at this height it must be at least 85 degrees F.

The *Naga* steps

Not everyone using the steps had enough stamina

It is time to head for lunch and a twenty-minute drive brings me to the Horizon Botanical Garden and Village. This is by the side of a busy road and appears to have been created out of nothing as the surrounding area is quite barren. It seems to be residential as well as catering for casual lunchers like today, and the surroundings are extremely attractive and restful; there are beautifully manicured lawns, palm trees and a covered walkway that gives some slight respite from the heat. There is the sound of tinkling water from small fountains and in the middle of a small pond a terracotta urn dribbles water onto some water lilies. Lunch is mostly cool food eaten in an air-conditioned room with views of the gardens outside; it is all very nice.

Time to move on and there are yet more interesting things to see. First is a handicraft village including a factory where they produce beautifully decorated paper umbrellas, definitely not for our seasons. The speed and skill of the workers in quite primitive conditions is remarkable. There are also some very colourful hanging tapestries in their finished product shop, and only two days into this holiday I have already started to

Horizon Botanical Garden and Village

acquire enough things to start me wondering about suitcase weight. As well as run-of-the-mill souvenir items there are some very attractive things to buy.

Next there is a short tour round a silk factory and I can follow the whole process from silk worm to silk dress. Some of the looms in here look as though they have come straight out of a Lancashire mill from about eighty years ago, the hands and feet of the women working them are in continual motion. A small and interesting fact I learned was that they can extract a five-hundred-metre length of silk from one cocoon about an inch long. The prices of the finished products seem quite expensive to me, although I do not have silk-buying experience and compared with UK prices they are probably pretty reasonable.

Outside there is an open but roofed area where workers sit on small stools surrounded by paints and brushes. The facilities are very poor with bare floor and little lighting and they each sit on unsafe-looking chairs with their board of designs on show; in addition to decorating products produced locally they also cater for tourists and will reproduce their art on any item you care to offer. There is no price list and they are shy about talking money so I make enquiries and it appears to be that the buyer should give what he/she thinks, but 50 baht is considered about the right amount. In this workshop they are prepared to paint designs on anything for you and they guarantee the finished article to be long lasting. A lady nearby opts for a butterfly on her t-shirt and it appears, as if by magic, in no time at all; it looks lovely.

I cannot resist having a dragon (although it is probably a *naga*) painted on the side of my camera bag and the whole thing only takes him about five minutes from start to finish. The result is truly excellent and so I give him 100 baht (about £1.60) which is twice what he would normally be offered. He is inscrutable and I get the feeling that that inscrutability would not change whether I offered him 50 or 500 baht. He is however happy to pose with my bag and his handiwork. With his skill, in a shop in the UK, I am sure that he would make a very comfortable living but he probably wouldn't be as happy as he is here. He tells me that his name is Guy; to me it does not seem a very Thai name but who can say.

Guy and my camera bag

There is also a lacquerware workshop and sale room but I decide to give that a miss and instead park myself on a high stool at an outside bar serving cold drinks. The young woman in charge is very multi-skilled as she effortlessly manages to hold a conversation with both me and a young man who appears to be more than a friend, while at the same time grinding ice and mixing coffee. Sitting under the shade of the bar sipping a delicious iced coffee in temperatures of about 90f seems to me to be a very pleasant way to spend your time.

It has been an interesting, enjoyable and busy day but it is still nice to relax and review my notes in the comfort of my air-conditioned room in the hotel. Another thing I learned today is that the Thai people are extremely fond of their royal family and will not accept any criticism of them. Everywhere you go there are large posters of the King and the rest of his family; they are on buildings, hoardings, roundabouts and even on specially constructed arches over roads. Many houses also have posters of them together with national and royal flags.

* * *

Another hot day dawns and there is an early start today as there is about an hour and a quarter drive to the Maeping Elephant Village where I will be able to have a ride on one of these wonderful pachyderms. It won't be my first ride as I did have that experience once before as a child of about eight during a visit to Chester Zoo, but that certainly wasn't through Thailand jungle and I have a sense of keen anticipation about it.

As we make our way through the suburbs of the city and through various road junctions I am struck by the number of small motorbikes that there are; this is more noticeable as we reach a red light at a junction where they are clustered in a great pack with the noise of their motors sounding like a lot of angry bees. When the lights change they depart like a swarm heading for the hive.

As we start to leave the city area it is still a wide road and its central reserve is filled with brightly coloured flowers that look a bit like petunias except that the range of colours and shades are much more exotic; there are lots of white oleanders as well. I have one of those at home but it steadfastly refuses to flower. On one side of the road there are shops selling all manner of things including bananas, tiles, bricks, terracotta work, chairs and timber as well as cafes, garden centres and motorbike repair shops (job for life there I should think).

The houses are thinning out a bit now and the mountains in the distance are covered in haze. In a field there is a long line of incredibly thin cows and there are now lots of banana trees. Passing through a small town I can see a house that is having building work done; it is surrounded by scaffolding made from bamboo and the whole thing looks very rickety indeed. There is a very large indoor market here and as we pass I can see that it is all vegetables and fruit. A motorbike passes on the other side obviously heading for the town; instead of a sidecar there is a table with a brightly covered top to which is attached a large umbrella and, incredibly, a bench seat. It is a complete and self-contained market stall.

There are more motorbikes, and one passes on the other side. It is obviously a family outing and the sequence is: a small child on the handlebars clutching a large bag, dad driving, daughter behind him with her arm round his waist and mother bringing up the rear. How they stay on beats me. I believe the record is five people on one motorbike.

For the last few minutes the countryside has been more remote and there are now lots of trees. Without warning we suddenly turn off the main road and bump down a track through the trees; we have arrived. This elephant training camp not only caters for tourists but is also a conservation and training camp for elephants that found themselves out of work after logging was mechanised. It takes about five years to train an elephant and during that time they learn how to carry, push and stack logs. The elephant is a national symbol in Thailand and although the performance of these tasks is now for the benefit of tourists, that income is a positive way of helping to ensure their survival.

The elephants are clustered round a raised platform and I gingerly step into the howdah tied on the back of one of them. I say gingerly because one slip and you are among the milling feet of about or eight or nine very large and heavy animals.

The first part of the trek is down to the river and we wade downstream for about half a mile; the river is about three or four feet deep at this point and it is very pleasant sitting high above the water with the trees down to the bank on each side. Leaving the river and climbing the bank you become aware of the elephant's somewhat exaggerated movement and it takes some concentration to stay in your seat, but up and on the level in the trees it is a very pleasant and restful experience made all the better by the different bird noises all around us. It is obvious that the mahout and his elephant have a good rapport as the occasional word or tweak on its ear always has an effect; it is almost a conversation without words.

There is a well-defined trail that the elephants have trodden many times. It follows a track high above a valley and then down across a stream until we reach the banana stop. This is a raised platform in a clearing manned by a woman who sells you a bunch of bananas to give to the elephant; there are about twenty in the bunch and they are scooped up in his trunk and vanish in one go. This is a situation enacted many times by the woman, the mahout and the elephant and your only role in this little routine is to supply the twenty baht for the bananas. What a bargain they were – I could have eaten a couple myself – singles not bunches!

Then it's up through the trees and down again, and across the river by a different route and back to the camp; the whole trip took about forty-five minutes and was highly enjoyable.

Next is the spectacle of elephant bath time, something that they enjoy immensely as they roll about in the river, sometimes with their legs in the air. When the mahout has given them a good scrub they come out

Heading up river

The banana stop

A jungle trail

Bath time

My new friend

of the river with a trunk full of water that they spray at anybody unwise enough to be too close. Another well-tried routine I am sure.

It is time for a display and there is a small grandstand where I can sit and watch the elephants perform the tricks and tasks that they have learned. These include all the tasks that they would have done as working elephants and also some tricks such as balancing on a log, walking on three legs and dancing a routine. One of the *mahouts* then sets up an easel with a palette of paints on a chair and gives one of the elephants a small paintbrush. It then proceeds to produce a credible painting of some flowers. It may or may not have had an outline to follow but it is still quite an achievement, and you can buy the finished product in their gift shop and museum.

Next is the raft trip down the river. It is only a short walk to where the rafts are all lined up against the bank; they are merely several large

The river Ping

Hat and scarf seller

Playing in the river

Loading the rafts

View from the bridge

bamboos tied together with a couple of raised planks that you sit on. I am glad that it is a placid river and that there is no white water involved.

The raft ride down the river Ping is another very enjoyable experience; there are no rapids or anything like that and the slowly flowing water in some places is only inches deep. The raft is guided by a man on the back with a long pole and when we occasionally 'ground' he gets off and gives us a push. There are actually four of us on the raft and the combined weight sometimes results in us getting our feet wet – well me anyway. It is very hot and the presence of water does not give any illusion of coolness, but it still very peaceful and relaxing to sit here and look at the trees that come down to the water. It is very quiet.

On one bank I can see some humpback cows placidly chewing the cud and in the trees there is a small wooden house on stilts. Two or three wooden carts with parasols are close by, their yokes resting in the dust, perhaps sheltering some produce from the sun. It looks an idyllic existence but probably only from my perspective. We round a bend and it is suddenly not so quiet, as there are two young boys having a wonderful time playing in the river. As if by a signal a young girl appears and wades out to meet our raft; she is laden with hats and scarves and intent on selling me one of them.

Soon it is all behind us and we have reached the point where the raft is dragged out of the river and loaded onto a trailer, with others, to go back for another journey. It was an extremely pleasant thirty minutes and looking back down the river from the bridge, I can see why. I must mention the bridge, as all along both sides there are different coloured bougainvillea planted in pots and the profusion of colour as they trail along the bridge is beautiful to see; there are also vivid red hibiscus and other coloured shrubs that I can't identify.

Boiling elephant dung

On the way to lunch we make a brief stop for a look round a small wayside industry where they manufacture items from elephant dung. The whole process from start to finish is carried out in a not so big building that is open on two sides; there is a series of stone troughs where, in turn, the dung is boiled, bleached, beaten and then put in water. Following this it is sieved, left to dry and then formed into paper. Outside there is a small monkey chattering in the branches of a tree but he is not interested in my blandishments and stares at me suspiciously. It is extremely hot in the building.

It is a bit too hot for me in the factory shop across the courtyard as well, so I opt for the shade of the spreading branches of a very large tree nearby. There is a display of finished products in the factory area and it is incredible what they make from this waste product, for I can see bathroom slippers, towel holders, tower dolls, oven mitts, appliance covers and picture frames. I am sure that there is a much more extensive range of items in their shop.

Following this not very appetising experience it is time to head for lunch and today this will be at a nearby orchid farm that also has a large restaurant area. At the orchid farm, or the Botanic Resort, Chiang Mai to give it its proper name, there is a lovely al fresco lunch waiting. Considering that I tend to try and restrict my eating at home, here in Thailand I find that I am ready for a full meal, usually of some sort of curry, at breakfast, lunch and dinner, and the amazing thing is that my waistband feels no tighter now than it did a week ago. Afterwards, it is delightful to wander round this rather special place and look at the lovely orchids that grow here. The whole area is laid out beautifully with the orchids growing under steel frames covered in netting; there

The orchid farm

are all sorts of different coloured orchids growing in neat little rows with their roots dangling down in the air.

Small paths weave around all the orchid houses and there are pools with little fountains and lots of palm trees, the whole pattern of things obviously designed to enhance the growing conditions. There is also a small area completely enclosed with netting; the environment in here is kept misty and humid and to get in there is a sort of airlock arrangement. In here butterflies fly free and there are several brown speckled ones sitting on some pineapple pieces, but they steadfastly refuse to open their wings for me to photograph them.

After a change of shirt back at the hotel I am off again, this time to Chiang Mai railway station as in the morning there will not be much time for wandering around and taking photographs. I had thought of walking but this seems a good opportunity for my first tuktuk ride, those three-wheeled taxis that seem to get all their own way on the road. I think they must get shooed away from the front of the hotel but it is easy to find one, and as we set off the ride is as alarming and exhilarating as I had always imagined it to be.

Chang Mai station

The driver is very talkative and asks me lots of questions about where I am from and why I have come to Thailand. He doesn't understand why I would want to come to his lovely city only to then leave it and take a 1700-mile train ride to Singapore. He comes from Lamphun, an ancient town a few miles away, and says that although his family are still there, it was too quiet for him and he moved to Chiang Mai. He certainly gets plenty of noise driving this thing round. When I ask him what cc the engine is he becomes confused and says he doesn't understand. I ask the question out of curiosity as I have heard that some of the tuktuk owners put 1000cc motorbike engines in what was already a lethal mode of transport. Perhaps this is what he has done as well. In addition to driving fast he has a disconcerting habit of turning round every so often to ask a question or make a point. There are no sides or doors to this vehicle and the tarmac that is whizzing past so fast seems only inches away.

The traffic increases and we come up behind a large Mercedes. At this moment I would bet a large amount of money that there isn't a gap between the Mercedes that we are coming up on and the parked car that he is overtaking, but my driver has no hesitation and we squeeze through. The driver turns round again, and gives me a big smile. I didn't see whether the Mercedes driver was smiling as well. My driver suddenly dives off to the right down a narrow cobbled road, or what seems like cobbles, and I am hurled from one side to the other whilst being bounced about, and then suddenly we have arrived. I part with 80 baht (about £1.30) and consider that it is a very small price for such an experience, for whatever I have just written, I did enjoy the ride. Unfortunately I forgot to ask him for a photograph of himself and his machine

Chiang Mai station is not far from the river and the large forecourt here is fairly empty except for a few tuktuk drivers hopefully waiting for a fare. The red tiled station building is long and low with an impressive white clock tower and in a corner some distance from the station there is a steam locomotive on a plinth. It is Swiss-built C56 class 2–8–0 locomotive number 340 and it gives the impression of having seen better days. Climbing into the cab I can see that everything that might have identified the type or manufacturer has been removed; the only thing remaining is the pressure gauge and that has no markings on it. My guess is that the loco is of 1940s, vintage, but it could well be much earlier.

An unidentified loco at Chang Mai station

There is a spacious and nicely tiled booking hall where I can get timetables, but first a cup of coffee in the station café. As the only European in there I come in for a few stares from the other customers but they soon lose interest and I sit and drink my iced coffee and watch the ebb and flow of Thai life around me.

The railway police have their own office here and when I approach them and ask for information they are very helpful and I end up with a fistful of leaflets and maps. The station is relatively quiet at the moment as there is just one local train due to depart in about fifteen minutes. The whole place is beautifully clean with no litter or graffiti and between the two main platforms is a very attractive garden with shrubs, flowers and a small lawned area.

In and around Chiang Mai station

The return journey by tuktuk is a bit less adventurous, but the driver still keeps up a fair speed and taking photos out of the back, while holding on, is a bit tricky. We are on one of the main routes back into the city and everywhere there is the snarl of motorbikes; from what I can see, most of them are ignoring the traffic lights when they are on red. Suddenly, on the other side of the road, I spot a very bright yellow car; it is a Trabant and the first one I have ever seen. These small cars were made in Saxony, which at the time was in East Germany; they were small and very light and had a smoky two-stroke engine, and although the car was notorious for its poor performance, more that three million of them were made. Following the fall of the Berlin wall in 1989 many families arrived in West Berlin with all their belongings piled into their Trabant.

I am back in my hotel room getting ready for dinner and I can see the sun setting behind a nearby hotel building, the mountains now just a shadow and the sun a great big orange globe. It is my last night in this very nice hotel and at dinner, from the usual varied selection of dishes, I choose roast duck curry with cashew nuts, lychees, pineapple and chillies. I follow this with pineapple tartlets, rum balls and iced coffee.

Another memory to take back from this part of Thailand is the Durian fruit that, although native to Malaya, is widely grown here. The fruits have a thick rough skin covered with spikes and come from trees that can grow up to 150 feet; it is very much a tropical tree and will not flourish if the daytime temperature falls below 70°F. The famous description of Durian fruit is that it tastes like heaven and smells like hell, but it is a great delicacy with many Asians. Because of its strong and pungent smell it is widely banned from hotels, airlines, public transport, hospitals and shops. Some of the smells attributed to it include rotted fish, stale vomit, unwashed socks, sewage, used surgical swabs and over-ripe cheese. Many places have signs forbidding this fruit, including this hotel.

Durian Fruit – Empress Hotel Chiang Mai

Here in northern Thailand people prefer the fruit to be as soft and pungent as possible but in some other parts of Asia people prefer it over-ripe when the flesh is richly creamy and a bit alcoholic. The taste is reminiscent of creamy, rich and highly flavoured custard with a hint of almonds and if you can get past the nauseating smell it is one of the great pleasures of fruit eating.

Morning. Thanking and saying goodbye to the restaurant and reception staff is like parting from old friends and I have only been here three days, such is the friendliness of these people. Chiang Mai is a place that I would visit again.

It is a fairly early start for the 08.45 train to Bangkok, a journey that will take twelve hours and which I am looking forward to very much. My luggage is going to the station separately in a little van bearing the legend 'Jatuchok express'.

Chiang Mai station is very busy this morning; there are people and food stalls everywhere and a twelve-coach train has just left. In its place there is a somewhat battered-looking local train that is going to Nakhon Sawan, its leather straps still gently swinging from the motion of the train pulling in. It might be a local train but it will still take eight hours to reach its destination.

The train for Bangkok pulls into another platform; it is a three-car sprinter type and has no sooner stopped than platform staff are all over it. There are people sweeping and cleaning inside, there is a man underneath the coaches with a torch, while on the platform there is a man with what looks like a 45-gallon drum on a set of pram wheels. There is a little petrol motor at the back that pumps water through a hosepipe and he is busy hosing down the train while a man with a long-handled brush follows him to complete the job.

Although there will be refreshments on the train, I decide that in the few minutes left I will supplement those with a tube of crisps, a can of iced coffee and a kilogram of fresh lychees in their shells that cost me about forty pence. I was later to discover later that everyone who joined

Girl with lychees

the train between here and Bangkok was given a meal, similar to that on an aeroplane.

Inside, the coach is clean and comfortable and as we pull out of the station spot on time I can see fuel tankers, goods wagons and lots of sidings. Chiang Mai is obviously an important railhead. The train follows a road for a short while but is soon in the countryside and it becomes very green with a lot of lychee and banana trees. There are also coconut palms and lots of different coloured bougainvillea. The fans fixed in the roof of the coach are all turning and whirring, and although they are just stirring warm air, the movement when it faces you, is very welcome. We pass a huge still pond that is covered with giant lily pads and beautiful big white flowers; it could be the lotus flower although as it disappears behind us we pass a similar pond where the flowers are a bright red. I have been steadily peeling and munching the lychees that I bought and the fruit inside is very white and fleshy and refreshing to eat.

It is now just about half an hour since we left Chiang Mai and we have reached Lamphun, a very pretty, busy and picturesque station with lots of flowers and shrubs on the various platforms. The ancient town that this station serves is where my tuktuk driver came from and is mainly wooden houses alongside the Kuang river, although there is a museum with some historically very interesting exhibits and an important temple called Wat Phra That Haripunchai. The station official in his smart uniform and with his flags, takes his duties very seriously in seeing the train start but he also has time for a smile when I wave to him.

Lamphun station

We have been clattering across latticework bridges over green and slow-moving rivers and it is now a very picturesque area with lots of indigenous trees and the mountains in the background. There is a beautiful mimosa tree, and looking ahead at this moment, the line gives the impression of heading straight into the jungle.

It is very relaxing sitting back in this comfortable train as we pass through this part of northern Thailand. Suddenly, the jungle recedes and we are passing through an area where there are lots of paddy fields that stretch away towards the mountains shimmering in the distance. A few minutes later and we have reached Nong Lom station, which has beautiful gardens and trees, including an enormously high tamarisk, and a very short platform so that only one coach of the train can be used; it doesn't appear on the timetable.

Nong Lom station

This line is single track to Bangkok and the only passing places are in stations, so we now have a few minutes to wait to let an intercity-type train pass on its way to Chiang Mai. There is again a railway official on the platform in a very smart light brown uniform and peaked cap; he is also armed with a red and a green flag to see the train safely through his station whether it stops there or not.

Not long after leaving Nong Lom we pass through another station without stopping. This is Patel Saelamaetha and close by there is a very rich and ornate pagoda covered in gold leaf. There are areas where a lot of work on the railway is in progress and this is mainly due to flooding and track damage caused by the torrents of water that cascade down the nearby mountains in the rainy season. We are crawling along at about 20mph and

Railway man at Nong Lom

have just crossed a newly built and concrete reinforced embankment with a new bridge; I can see the remains of the old embankment which has been washed into the river in the valley below.

The importance of this line is obvious not only from the quality of the track but also from the reconstruction and protection of it with reinforced embankments and concrete gullies to take away the flood water. At the moment there are six trains a day each way between Bangkok and Chiang Mai, and while this one will take twelve hours, there are two that take in excess of fourteen hours and obviously cater for all the stations that we are not scheduled to stop at. My timetable shows eighteen stations between Chiang Mai and Bangkok but there are many more than that on this line.

The view soon becomes one of thick woods again and there are lots of mimosas. The track is continually twisting and turning as it follows the contours of the mountains and climbs higher and we pass through another station without stopping; it is Khun Tan. This station is the gateway to Doi Khun Tan National Park which covers an area of about 255 square kilometres; it was opened in 1975 and straddles the mountains that separate the provinces of Lamphun and Lampang. Somewhat surprisingly the park's most renowned feature is that here is the longest railroad tunnel at 1352 metres.

In the past the park used to be home to bears, tigers, elephants, wild cattle, gibbons and lots of other species, but hunting, logging and human encroachment have meant that they have all gone. Wild life today in the park is mainly weasel, Siamese hare, porcupine and wild boar as well as various birds, reptiles and insects. The lowland part of the park used to be a teak forest but that has gone as well.

About ten kilometres from Khun Tan station is the Mae Long Waterfall with its year-round cascade of sparkling water. Almost immediately after the station we enter the tunnel and when we emerge it is into very thick jungle where the bamboos must be at least fifty feet high. This train and its tracks are the only evidence that human beings have passed this way and I am sure that you would only have to walk a hundred yards from the track to get lost.

Suddenly we pass over a very high bridge and there is a drop of about two hundred feet on each side; the suddenness of it after the closeness of the trees is a bit startling. The view is constantly changing and although it is still jungle there are areas where local people have slashed and burned areas near to the railway and planted banana trees and rice.

Another station appears and falls behind; it was Hang Chat and there are now large areas of rice growing. In a field I can see some of the thinnest cows that I have ever seen.

It is just over two hours since we left Chiang Mai and we have now reached Nakhon Lampang, which is a town situated along the Wang river. It is a place of no little importance and there is a profusion of sidings and rail oil tankers, and what looks like a refinery as well. It is the second largest town in northern Thailand and is a very busy trading centre; it is also a good base for travel around northern Thailand. In the nineteenth century the town became a teak production centre; most of the workers were from Burma and the teak houses and Burmese-style temples throughout the town reflect their influence. Teak furniture is still one of the traditional crafts produced here today. Another interesting and unique thing about Lampang is the horse carriages; there are about fifty of these brightly coloured horse-drawn vehicles and they form the main transport around the town, particularly for tourists like myself.

The train departure is again a very organised affair and one of the station officials with a flag is joining the train here. As we pull away he is happy to talk about himself and his job: he has worked on this railway since he left school and has been promoted twice and is now a senior platform inspector along the line. He has a son who he hopes will join the railway as he says it is an organisation that appreciates and takes care of its staff and there is good job security. He is very interested in the fact that I travel on railways around the world and asks me many questions; he is amazed that I was allowed to travel on the carriage roof and the locomotive tender in Ecuador.

After Nakhon Lampang we pass through a succession of immaculate stations with their brown and cream buildings and attractive gardens,

Lampang – I forgot to ask his name

always with the smart official and his flags. Some of the ones that I manage to note are Mae Tha, Salphafla Hat, Mae Mo, Mae Chang, Pang Puai and Pha Kho. We stop at Pang Puai to exchange the single line token and also to let an express through on its way to Chiang Mai. This is another attractive station surrounded by trees and jungle and as we wait it is very pleasant listening to the birds outside over the noise of the gently throbbing train engines. We wait here about fifteen minutes until suddenly with a whoosh and a rattle the express flashes past on the other track and we are on our way again.

Pang Puai station

Between Pang Puai and the next station, Pha Kho, the line enters a very thickly wooded and tropical area where the bamboos have trunks as thick as my arm. Suddenly at the lineside, in an area where there seems to be no human habitation of any sort, there is a small grave surrounded by a little white fence with an enormous white cross that has toppled over and droops sadly over the grave. I wonder who is in that solitary cemetery in this very remote spot, and why.

Apart from where the small villages are and where some of the tribes have slashed and burned to create space to grow a few bananas and vegetables, it remains a thickly wooded area, and it is a delight to be transported through this very pleasant vista in the comfort of this train as it continues to twist and turn its way up through the mountains with the occasional squeal from the wheels as it takes a tight curve. Lunch is served and is a sort of spaghetti bolognese with salad followed by a pudding with cream; the pudding is a bit like green tapioca but is very sweet and delicious. There are also fresh buns with coffee and water and it is all included in the very reasonably priced ticket.

Ban Pin station

We pass through Ban Pin and the view changes yet again, this time to a high bridge over a broad river that sweeps away across the valley; in the distance I can see a quarry and a huge slash in the mountain where the product has been extracted. This view is soon replaced by a broad cultivated plain that is covered in paddy fields where I can see workers harvesting the rice crop.

It is four hours since we left Chiang Mai and we reach Den Chai where there is a large oil refinery and lines of tankers parked in a vast rail yard. Among some trees nearby I can see a derelict water tower from steam-hauled days; this is part of the ever-changing view that I have had since we started, which has included banana and lychee plantations, rice fields, areas of slash and burn, thick jungle, rural villages and towns, quarries, and wooded mountains.

We arrive at Sila At station, which is much more modern and functional-looking than those I have seen so far, and looking beyond the station I can see some three-storey housing blocks. It is only a brief stop and we are then under way again; just outside the station there is a reminder of the steam locomotive days with a faded green and black 4–6–2 locomotive on a plinth. Its number is 274.

No. 274, Sila At station

The timetable shows the next station as Uttaradit but in effect one town runs into another. The whole area is a picture of industry with rail wagons, office buildings and houses; the main temple here is Wat Tha Thanon and it is just behind the station. Inside there is a bronze Lanna Buddha. Uttaradit's most famous citizen is King Taksin who was born here in the eighteenth century. It was he who reunited Thailand after the Burmese sacked Ayutthaya in 1767. Within a few minutes of leaving Uttaradit it is just a memory, with now just the odd house on stilts surrounded by trees and small banana plantations.

House on stilts

The train staff are now very busy again as everybody who joins this train is served with a meal and a drink. The view soon changes again and we are getting into an area where rice is grown in earnest; here there is a permanent water supply and there are acres and acres of waving green rice stretching out to the horizon.

A woman with a young child of about four is now sitting across from me. The woman does not speak any English but returns my smile; a smile is a lovely greeting in any country and does not need any words to convey friendship. With just smiles and gestures we share with pleasure the antics of her young son who is clearly enjoying the journey as he crosses from side to side of the carriage to see what he can see outside. He finally flops into his seat and fixes me with an unwinking stare from his wide and clear brown eyes; his expression does not change even when I offer him some of my lychees, until his mother says something and his little fist instantly plunges into the proffered bag. I take a picture of him with my digital camera and then, with the air of a conjuror, I show him the result. He clearly sees it as some kind of wonderful trick and, as he looks at his picture, his face is wreathed in smiles. I only wish that my camera had been Polaroid so that I could give him a picture to take home.

The waving fields of rice have now given way to jungle again and we are passing a small village with a dirt road meandering through it on its way into the jungle; there is nobody to be seen.

A jungle village

We pass a station which I think was called Bang Kon and nearby there were people laying out rice on the concrete, presumably to dry. I have worked out that although there are only thirteen stations we are scheduled to stop at between Chiang Mia and Bangkok, there are many others we don't stop at that are served by local trains. There is a station about every eight to ten miles, some of them with quite exotic gardens.

It is 3.30 and we have arrived at Phitsanulok, which is big, busy, functional and modern with lots of people about and many market stalls. In the station there are several platforms and it is busy with people waiting for trains while others are trying to sell them drinks, fruit and anything else that they think the traveller may, or may not, need. Many visitors and travellers pass through Phitsanulok as it is more or less in the geographical centre of northern Thailand and is a crossroads between Chiang Mai in the north, Khon Kaen in the east, Bangkok in the south and the Myanmar border in the West. There are several railway people clustered round the train and it appears that there is something wrong with one of the engines. There is a lot of talk and arm-waving, the result of which is that one man couples up a hosepipe and then proceeds to hose down the engines with cold water – so much for technology.

Phitsanulok Station

Not long after leaving Phitsanulok and we are again travelling through a vast rice-growing area. From my notes, this view went on for about two hours and I saw nothing else but different shades of rice growing. There are though lots of pagodas here and there and several lovely little towns along the way; most of the houses are built on stilts, presumably for when the wet season arrives.

A fairly large town and station appears and recedes – it is Ta Phah Kim; there is a lot of poverty on the lineside here. A sluggish and uninviting-looking green river follows the railway at this point and the houses on stilts that are built alongside it are very poor looking.

The train is now back travelling through the vast rice fields where there is nothing else as far as the eye can see. Suddenly there is a station

Do not shoot the birds notice

in the middle of this with not a sign of habitation anywhere; remarkably it also is staffed, as well as having the ubiquitous man with the green flag waving us through. It's nearly six o'clock and the sun is going down as a great burning orb. We are now running about fifty minutes late, which means that it will be properly dark when we reach the next station at Lop Buri.

Lop Buri is one of Thailand's oldest cities with a thriving modern town east of the old city and as we pull into the station I can see a market; it is very busy and the twinkling lights of the stalls give it a slightly magical air. There are many ancient temples and buildings here, some of which go back a thousand years. Perhaps the most typical is Prang Sam Yot which was originally built as a Hindu shrine and later renovated as a Buddhist temple, with its three phallic towers (*prangs*) and wonderfully preserved stonework; it is an impressive sight and well worth a visit.

We are now about two hours away from Bangkok and running into Ayutthaya. Here on the outskirts of the town is a sight that I have not seen so far. There are single-storey houses all along the side of the track and the majority of them have only three sides with the open side facing the railway, so that as the train slowly rolls past you are treated to a brief look at family life in each of them: a family sitting down to the evening meal, two young men playing cards, a small child in a tin bath being washed by his mother. It is a moving vista of family life and in the two- or three-foot gap between the train and the houses there are many young children playing in the dust.

Ayutthaya became the most powerful kingdom in Siam in the fourteenth century and by the middle of the sixteenth century ruled most of what is now Thailand. Its end came when it was sacked by Burma in 1767 after many years of simmering conflict, and at that time many of the beautiful buildings of the period were razed to the ground by the Burmese. Today, Ayutthaya has some of the most spectacular ruins in Thailand and although few examples of the Ayutthayan craftsmanship survived 1767, the Chao Sam Phraya Museum on Rotchana Road does have some examples of their work in bronze and gold.

After eleven hours on this train I am slightly surprised that I still feel comparatively fresh, although I am looking forward to the five-star luxury of the Bangkok Eastin Hotel.

We have just drifted through Bang Pa-in; this is very much a town of the latter nineteenth century but it does have a beautiful pavilion in the middle of an ornamental lake that was built in 1876 for Chulalongkorn, who ruled there from 1868 to 1910.

Without warning the scene outside changes, almost brutally, to roads, cars, shops, cafes and neon lights; we have reached the outskirts of Bangkok. As we pass through Bang Sue junction there is a general stirring among the passengers in anticipation of journey's end in about twenty minutes.

Getting off the train the heat hits you in the face and almost immediately I feel as though I need a cold drink and a shower, although there is a coach a short distance away and the air-conditioned ride to my hotel is very pleasant. The hotel lives up to its billing and is big, modern, spacious and cool with lots of marble. My room is extremely nice and well appointed and could probably sleep at least six people without any loss of comfort. A quick wash, followed by coffee and bed seems the order of the day. In the bathroom the wall-to-wall mirror is one of those that I describe as 'one that doesn't take any prisoners' and it accurately reflects the fact that I have been sitting in a warm train in the same clothes for the last thirteen hours.

Bangkok, Thailand's capital city, at 5.30 am on a Sunday morning, with the clouds starting to clear and the promise of another hot day. From my fifteenth-floor window I am looking across at a six-lane expressway and it is already extremely busy. Almost under my window is a suburban railway line and towering over it like a long concrete umbrella is part of the newly constructed sky train system which allows you to avoid the frantic congestion of this sprawling, bustling, congested and exciting city of fifteen million people.

Breakfast over at 8.30 am and I am off to Chinatown, which is situated between the main railway station and the Chao Phraya river. The narrow streets of Chinatown are packed with shops and markets and even on this Sunday morning it is a bustling, lively place; fighting your way through you are besieged by loud noise, movement and the smell of noodles.

I get the impression that you could probably buy anything here. There are over a hundred shops selling gold. There are stalls piled high with different spices of more colours than a rainbow and the smell and colour of them is intoxicating. Here, there is also Nakorn Kasem, or as it is perhaps better known, The Thieves Market. It is said that you can come here on a Sunday morning and buy back what you had had stolen the week before.

The first Chinese arrived in Thailand some eight hundred years ago and quickly integrated into their new country, and today there are some four million living in Bangkok.

I go back to the hotel for a change of shirt and from my bedroom window I can see a railway station that I have identified as Makkasan. I can also see an ancient-looking diesel locomotive and four old steam locomotives, two of which are 0–6–0s and would appear to date from the early 1900s, all standing on grass-covered tracks. They have obviously seen better days. I decide to go and investigate. The traffic on the expressway has gone from being extremely busy to what is now a seemingly never ending merry-go-round of cars. The window of my room is not conducive to good photographs but it will be my only opportunity to get these views.

There is a footway across the railway line and also a designated way across the building site under the sky train construction site. As I cross what seems to be a public road on the other side to get a closer look

Makkasan station

High-rise traffic

at these old engines a man appears seemingly out of thin air and furiously waves me away; he does not appear to have any objection to me taking photographs of these engines, just to my actual presence. He is clearly an official of some sort and it is not possible to reason with him and I retreat to a seat on the station platform. This is clearly a busy commuter line and several trains pass in the ten or fifteen minutes that I sit here; a Prachinburi to Bangkok service arrives and it is absolutely packed.

Watching the trains go by

Just outside and backing onto the railway there is a market in full swing with predominately carp and vegetables on sale. There is an overpowering smell of fish as I walk round the close-packed stalls and although the open areas between them are covered, their shade is illusionary as it is mega hot under them.

It is a fascinating slice of Thai life but I am not sorry to leave it behind for the shade of the trees that line the pavement along this road.

Thai Labour museum

Bikes only, please

The fish market

Fruit and vegetable market

The lake near the market

He was quick!

Just along the street is the Thai Labour museum, which has a collection detailing the evolution of Thai labour from the time that slavery existed up to the present. Across the front of the museum there is a monument to the dignity of labour; it is a stucco sculpture of two workers, a man and a woman, pushing an historical wheel.

As I make to cross the road to photograph what appears to be a rather nice lake, a small lizard darts out of a bush and just as quickly darts back again but not before I have managed to take a picture of him.

Next stop, and fortunately not on foot, is the Grand Palace which is a must-see for anyone visiting Bangkok. The road from Chinatown follows the river and past a statue of King Buddhayodfa the Great, situated by a bridge that was built in 1932 and carries his name. It was the second bridge to be built over this river, the first being the railway bridge built in 1922.

Near the bridge is Saphan Phut pier and where there is a great view of the longtail boats that ply up and down this river; you can hire one for about twenty pounds an hour but I am not doing that today. With their long sweeping prow high out of the water and the snarling engine driving them along the surface at tremendous speeds, they are an exciting sight.

It is only a short distance to the Grand Palace; this sprawling compound contains many ornate pavilions and shrines and also the Temple of the Emerald Buddha, Thailand's most important religious image. It was originally constructed as a city within a city, as a residence for the king and also for some government offices; it is completely surrounded by a very high wall which is over a mile all round. This magnificent layout was built by King Buddhayodfa the Great, the first King of the Chakri Dynasty and work started in 1782 after he decided that his palace at Thonburi on the other side of the river was not suitable.

Kinnon, a mythological creature half bird, half man

Ramakien figure

From the kerbside the Grand Palace looks unchanged, but outside it is very different as the compound is now surrounded by very busy roads and there are hundreds of people both in the palace and, like me, waiting to cross the road. There is a policeman stationed in the middle of the road; he is not very tall but he exudes authority; standing there in his tight-fitting helmet and leather boots he controls pedestrians and drivers alike with a baton and a steely glare. With a small gesture he suddenly stops the traffic and a nod of the head is enough to instruct us to cross; we surge to the other side like a tidal bore.

There are a lot of people inside, and the staff at the entrance to the palace are very strict on dress code: no bare legs or shoulders. A woman protests and says that she should not have to wear a top over her shoulders, which are bare except for her dress straps, but there is no choice, either she wears the proffered shawl or she does not get in. It is very hot walking around these fascinating buildings and wherever possible I am keeping to the shade.

Amarindra Winitchai Hall

The Royal Pantheon

The Amarindra Winitchai Hall was built in 1785 during the reign of King Rama I. It is used for state ceremonies such as the birthday anniversary of the King. The main feature is a throne surmounted by a white canopy and backed by a boat-shaped altar. The Chakri Maha Prasat was built by King Rama V in 1882 and has a throne room and two wings, nowadays mainly used for entertaining foreign ambassadors. The west side of the scripture library is said to be the finest in Bangkok. It has been a fascinating stroll round this complex with its intricate, artistic and beautiful buildings and it brings the day nicely to a close.

The Chakri Maha Prasat

The scripture library

Another new day, 5.30 am, and it promises to be very hot again. The traffic below my hotel window is an already solid three lines with many others trying to join from side roads. I am looking forward to today with all sorts of emotions, as there is an opportunity to visit Kanchanaburi to see the war graves of those who died building the Thailand–Burma rail link. There will also be a ride on the actual railway over the river Kwai bridge and across the wooden viaduct at Wang Pho, built by British prisoners of war.

The coach threads its way out of the city traffic and we are now on a dual carriageway. We pass a roadside shop selling life-size models of tigers, lions and horses; it would be nice to have a large garden with a few of those dotted about. The monotony of the straight road through the continuing built-up area is suddenly broken and we pass through what I am told is a good grape- and coconut-growing area; there are thick plantations of palm trees on one side of the road. We are now about 30 miles from Bangkok and apart from that one place where there were a lot of coconut palms, the area has been pretty much built-up all the way. There is a touch of interest as we pass a large building on the right. I am not sure what the building is for but on the top of it there is a gigantic yellow and green duck, presumably made from plaster; it must be at least 20 feet high and considerably more than that in length. A pick-up truck suddenly appears and races past us in a cloud of dust. In the back sprawled out on some sacking is a young man wearing a very bright yellow t-shirt with a motif on the front: 'King's 80th birthday'.

We are now just a few miles from the Thailand–Burma Railway Centre

Museum at Kanchanaburi and tree-covered mountains are now appearing on the left, the main product from this area is sugar cane. Kanchanaburi is the hottest province in Thailand with temperatures that can reach over 110 degrees Fahrenheit. The town itself is a very busy built-up place where all the shops crowd in on the main street that runs through it. Stepping off the coach outside the war cemetery I am immediately

The cemetery entrance at Kanchanaburi

Plaque commemorating those who died building the Thailand–Burma railway

A very emotional place

Neatly kept war graves

struck by the immaculately kept graves, the beautifully mown lawns and a large tree with great spreading branches that stands in the middle.

The museum is just across the road, and as I walk through its many galleries it is a journey through the history of the railway from its inception to its demise; this journey is made more poignant by the many relics from wartime camps that are on display here. Back across the road to the cemetery, and it is extremely hot walking along row after row of these neatly kept graves. I find it quite emotional looking at all the names and ages of those that lie here; some of the ages are 24, 28, 29,

Converted lorry and trailer

Locomotive outside River Kwai Bridge station

23, 25, 24 and 22. I reflect on what a waste of young lives the whole thing was. I can only guess at the emotion that any veteran walking round here might feel.

On to the station for a good look round before the train arrives; it is very busy and there are a lot of people on the bridge taking photographs. This is actually River Kwai Bridge station, as Kanchanaburi station proper is some distance back up the line. There are some interesting transport relics here from another age including a lorry and trailer converted to run on rails.

Walking onto the bridge it seems as though every inch is taken up with people walking backwards and forwards. There is a group of what seem to be army cadets and without any prompting from me they surge round for a photograph. They look a bit serious in the photograph but before that there was much hilarity and many questions.

On this wide and placid river, with its lush green background and mountains, there are floating restaurants and dragon boat trips; there is a happy feel about this beautiful place. It is impossible to imagine how

You're in the army now

River Kwai with bridge and dragon boat

it must have looked all those years ago with young British soldiers dying in intolerable conditions trying to construct this railway. I wonder what they would make of it today with tourists and locals alike travelling up and down on it. Perhaps they would be proud, as it is a testament to their courage and endurance.

River Kwai restaurants

I make my way back to the platform as the train is nearly due. There are two delightful little girls wandering up and down selling small bags of nuts. They are not doing very well and as I don't want any nuts I give them a donation instead, equivalent to about three bags or 15 pence in sterling. It seems a very small amount, but they are pleased.

The nut sellers

There is the sound of a locomotive whistle and as the train steams into view with its lovely rake of old wooden-seated carriages, an old man appears from the shade. He seems very frail and leans heavily on his companion. Unlike everyone else he is in no hurry. Following his appearance there is a

'Hellfire Pass', Kannyu

Wooden viaduct at Wang Pho, 1943

Completed railway at Konkoita

Allied prisoner of war cemetery at Kui Yae

Bridges over the river Kwai, December 1945

murmuring from people nearby and I learn that he is 91 years old and a veteran from the building of this railway. He has made this journey every year since the end of the Second World War, and his strength of purpose and homage to his former comrades is something to marvel at. Who can possibly know what his feelings are when he comes each year. I want to take his photograph but there is no opportunity to ask him, and I feel that it would be an intrusion to 'snap' him without asking.

The train is now travelling along at a good speed and all around is a vast fertile plain, which is highly cultivated. The forest-covered mountains in the background march away towards Burma and look very green.

Beautiful hills of Burma

The line is almost dead straight and has been like that for last twenty minutes. There have been huge paddy fields that have now given way to field after field of tapioca; the soil is a rich orangey brown colour. The first stop is at Thakilen, quite a big station, and a lot of people get on. As we rattle along there is still mile after mile of tapioca until we reach Lumsum and here there are many tall papaya trees with green pendulous fruits and a solitary passenger to get on.

Thakilen Station

Lumsum Station

Taking photos at Wang Pho

Approaching the viaduct

On the Wang Pho viaduct

We are now closely following the river and approaching the wooden viaduct built against the cliff face at Wang Pho that, by any standards, was a remarkable achievement by the prisoners of war who built it. We pass over the viaduct, which is a mass of criss-crossed railway sleepers held together by sections of railway line, and just on the other side there is what seems to be a station just for people visiting the viaduct; there are many stalls selling souvenirs and food. The old man gets off here as he has done many times before; he now has a long walking stick but appears rejuvenated.

Wang Pho station proper is a short journey further on and is where

Wang Pho Station

we are getting off. The line terminates at Nam Tok about ten miles further on, which at the time of the railway's construction was called Tha Sao and was the site of a large hospital camp where a thousand men died.

I have enjoyed this part of my journey very much, despite the sadness associated with what happened here. I hope that the men who lived and died here got at least some satisfaction from what they constructed, which today gives interest and pleasure to many.

From the station there is a very short walk through the trees to a restaurant with a bamboo roof, for lunch, followed by a road journey back to Bangkok.

Early start today for a visit to the Rose Garden Riverside. This delightful place is about an hour's drive away from Bangkok but in terms of surroundings and atmosphere it is a world away. Leaving the city you get some idea of its congestion problems as there are five lanes of traffic leaving the city and five lanes going the other way. Even beyond the city limits the roads are still busy but there are plenty of palm trees and colourful bougainvillea to brighten the view. We also pass a huge garden centre where there are rows and rows of potted roses and oleanders for sale. The road now crosses the Tha Chin river on a very wide bridge. I can see lots of lilies and a carpet of green leaves in the river and the whole mass gently sways with the movement of the water. We turn off the major road and the area becomes more rural; there are lots of trees with bright orange leaves; this is Pet Kasem Road. A few miles further on there is a sign that says: Rose Garden Riverside Hotel, Restaurant, Arusaya Spa, Rim Klong Market, Thai Cultural centre.

Rose Garden fountain

The Rose Garden has developed from the vision of one man, Doctor Chamnan Yupapurna, who in 1962 purchased a small piece of land on the bank of the river Ta Chine in order to own and rescue a bullet tree that was in danger of falling into the river because of erosion of the river bank. He also thought it would make a nice retreat for his wife and children. Today that vision is carried on by his family and this seventy-acre park is a living community of some five hundred people who preserve, maintain and develop this microcosm of historical Thai life. It is a glimpse into the past to see how the Thai people used to live.

The driveway from the road is delightful as there are oleanders, jasmine, and golden shower trees in bloom as well as small coloured shrubs.

The reception building also houses a large air-conditioned dining hall that overlooks a lake with a spouting fountain; it looks very cool out there through the tinted glass but it is actually extremely hot. There is a truly international selection of dishes served buffet style and it is a very pleasurable experience to ponder over all the delicious-looking meals and to savour the different aromas. It is very busy and most of the tables are taken.

On the other side of the lake there is a large Chinese pavilion and some typical Thai houses. In order to preserve original Thai houses, the owners of the park purchased some and re-erected them here alongside the lake; they are about a century old and are built on stilts and totally without nails.

People come here for many reasons, perhaps just for lunch, or a holiday, or to see traditional Thai life or perhaps just to unwind from modern living for a few hours. Whatever the reason I am sure that they achieve it here.

The lake

Wandering around the gardens, and trying to keep in the shade, I can see a profusion of orchids, roses and bananas and also some tall orangey-red flowers with very dark-green leaves that I am not able to identify. There are many interesting trees here as well, some of them really large specimens, including acacia, flame trees, rain trees, mahogany, wattle, golden shower and jasmine, and many others I am sure. All the gardens are beautifully maintained but I suppose they would be, as this place employs more than sixty gardeners. In conversation with one of them I learn that this is also a botanical park with a full-time botanist; he says that his whole family work here and it is one big community where everyone knows everyone else.

The beautiful gardens

Century-old Thai house

I have reached the river and here is the Pae Suan Sampran floating restaurant. It appears to be closed but the seating area built out over the water is still available for anyone wanting to just sit and relax and I head there for a five-minute break from the relentless sun. As I approach, there is a great scurry and splash and something large disappears from the reeds at the edge and into the river; it could have been anything. Doctor Yupapurna's river is very wide at this point and there are great clumps of weed gently floating downstream with the current; it is very restful sitting here.

Ta Chine river

I continue my exploration of this very attractive and exotic place and after pausing for a while under the cool shade of a big spreading mango tree, I wander off through some trees and suddenly come across a small lake, more of a pond really. There are three boats on it laden with fresh fruit with a traditionally dressed Thai woman in each one. I'm not sure if the fruit is for sale or whether it is just to depict a typical river market; either way it makes a nice photograph.

Floating market

They weigh about the same

I am heading for the elephant enclosure, but on the way there is a man with several brightly coloured macaws and cockatoos; they are perched on a rail and none of them are chained in any way and are obviously quite tame. For 40 baht I can have my photograph taken with a cockatoo on my head, one on my chest and two macaws, one sitting on my arm and the other hanging by his beak on my finger. I feel slightly ridiculous standing here covered in brightly coloured birds but the closeness of these exotic creatures is nevertheless a pleasurable experience.

Arriving at the elephant enclosure where there is to be a demonstration of their working capabilities, I am greeted by a man with an extremely long white python draped around him. He says that its name is Charlie and he is anxious that I have a photograph of myself with Charlie draped around my neck, but I make my excuses and depart into the adjacent souvenir shop. There is a large concrete area outside and the elephants tethered at the side of it are shuffling their feet and flapping their huge ears, the mahouts sitting motionless astride them. It is as if they are all waiting for some sort of signal.

There is a sudden shout and a flurry of activity as the elephants give the crowd a demonstration of how to push, carry and stack logs just as they would have done in the jungle years ago before logging was either mechanised or made illegal. At the end of the arena there is a deep pool of water and one of the elephants shows us how they can retrieve floating logs.

It is an enjoyable spectacle watching the elephant and mahout working as one, but I can't help reflecting that the elephants in Chiang Mai had a better deal with a river to splash in and a jungle to walk through, although in both cases the tourist money is essential to their future and their well-being.

There is now about an hour or so before it is time to return to Bangkok, enough to be able to watch the Thai Village cultural show. After the heat outside it is a bit of a relief to enter the large auditorium next to the elephants, a very large and high wooden building with wooden seats round three sides, rather like an amphitheatre. The auditorium represents a typical Thai village with the central clay area as the village square, and the stage represents the inside of a typical Thai house found in the countryside.

The Thai folklore floor show

The scene opens with the residents of the village waking to the sun and a new day; a woman is singing gently to her baby. Next, the beautiful young girls of the village perform the Nagee Saran dance; this dance is to the Water Spirit who will provide rain so that the farmer will be able to plant his crops. They are all dressed in traditional bright-blue costumes with little gold-coloured pointy hats. Rice is Thailand's main crop and at harvesting time they perform the harvest dance as a reward for the hard work of the previous year. In front of me the central clay area is a whirling mass of young men and women in brightly coloured clothes dancing with obvious enjoyment to the insistent and loud music.

When the harvesting is finished and there is little to do, the young men practise Glong Sabutchai or Victory Drums. At this time there are also various other activities such as Thai boxing, sword fighting and pole fighting, and down in the central area a demonstration of Thai boxing is taking place. It is remarkably realistic and there is an underdog, plainly playing to the crowd. The bout eventually ends with the underdog laying out the umpire and the match being declared a draw. This is followed by several young men demonstrating sword fighting and pole fighting; their choreography and timing is a joy to watch.

All these activities have been played against a background of very insistent music that sounds very like that which comes from a snake charmer's pipe. In this representation of village life at this time many young men and women meet in the village square with thoughts of courtship and marriage, and following the ceremony in the bride's house the whole village joins in the celebrations and there is much dancing to entertain the guests.

The whole ensemble is now present and we are treated to a colourful and extravagant finale with four dances from the four main regions of Thailand. First, there is the intricate and lively Bu-Nga welcome dance, which represents the south; next, the slow and graceful northern Fingernail dance; followed by the elegant central region Vichanee dance with its exquisitely crafted fans. Finally, there is the boisterous north-eastern Bamboo dance, which signifies camaraderie; in this dance young men and women dance continually through an arch while trying to avoid the clashing bamboos of those on either side.

I think the idea of preserving this microcosm of Thai life is an excellent one, and this show, fully representative of that idea, is both very interesting and enjoyable from start to finish. A fitting end to the day before I leave Thailand tomorrow.

This is the end of my journey through Thailand, at least for the time being, and everything that I have seen, done and heard has been very enjoyable, I have particularly enjoyed the food: I even had, and enjoyed, beef and potato mussaman curry for breakfast on one occasion. It is not for everyone though. There have been new and exciting experiences and I have found the people friendly and helpful. The country is varied and interesting to travel through: it is indeed the land of smiles.

The timings are a bit tight this morning for catching the day/night train to Kuala Lumpur, so there is only just time for one quick picture of the outside of Bangkok station. I notice along the way, as we pass a wide canal, that redundant bogies from old railway coaches have been utilised as seating along the water's edge: they look good and not at all out of place, if a little unusual.

Bangkok station this morning is a big, bustling, busy place with at least ten railway lines entering the glass and steel-domed station; all the lines have passenger trains, some local and some long distance. There are virtually no western European people on the platform.

Bangkok station

The train that I am catching is from platform 5, but first there is a lot of shunting of carriages in and out of that platform. It seems a little strange to be doing that when the train is due out shortly, but who knows. There is no gentle joining of carriages here, as they are just slammed together. It is baking hot and, as I stand wilting, I reflect that you could make a lovely tropical garden under the high glass roof.

The train is eventually sorted out and I get into conversation with one of the railwaymen who has been checking on the carriage couplings. He seems to think it will be at least another hour before the train leaves, and as I start thinking about going outside for another photo. He then says that maybe it will leave very soon. The moment passes as he asks me why I am in Bangkok and where I am going; the opportunity to talk with him is much more valuable than a second photo. He is delighted to have his picture taken.

A happy railway man

The long train eventually snakes its way out of the station and although it is considerably late in leaving, it doesn't seem to matter.

Goodbye Bangkok

Passing by

The journey through the suburbs seems to take an age, but suddenly it is slightly more rural and almost immediately lineside dwellings appear; the scene is slightly reminiscent of my journeys along South American railway lines. As we crawl past, their whole world is there for us to see; the quality of the clothing hanging on some of the washing lines does not always match the quality of the building.

Life along the line

Railside washing line

We reach Bang Sue Junction; this is an important junction as it is from here that all the trains to the south of the country depart. The view now becomes more rural and cultivated, and bananas and coconuts seem to be the main crop; there are still a few habitations alongside the railway. Small industrial towns with their own station come and go, and the coconuts and bananas now give way to vast expanses of rice.

Bang Sue Junction

There is very little change with the view and I decide to settle down and catch up with my notes of the journey so far. Sometime during the night we will pass through Hua Hin, which was the old Royal Capital of Thailand.

Sweet dreams

* * *

I have a very relaxed night and although asleep I was also conscious of the movement of the train, which swayed very slowly all night. I get up and stroll down the still-sleeping carriage to the door, which I can open. I'm not sure what time it is but I can see that we have arrived at a station called Chumphon which, according to my timetable, we should have reached at 21.47 last night! From some notes that I made about this place I can see that it is the gateway to the southern border towns of Thailand and that it has some lovely and unspoilt beaches.

It is now 5.45 am and dawn is breaking. We pass through a station called Chaiya; there are a lot of people waiting for a local train. Standing at the open door I can see trees and fields slowly taking shape in the morning light. Even without weather-forecasting skills, I can see that it is going to be another very hot day. At 6.10 am we stop at Surat Thani which according to my timetable we should have reached at a quarter to one this morning; we are five and a half hours late! Although there are a lot of corrugated iron and bamboo shacks near the railway, the town itself is big and is obviously an important centre.

The view now gives way to extensive forestry and is also a place where a lot of snakes are found; slowly but surely the cultivated forest gives way to a very tropical forest. Still in this very tropical area we reach Thung Song, which is a railway junction. From here you can get a train to the popular resort of Phuket on the west coast of Thailand. It is also a large and attractive town and a lot of the houses have bright terracotta roof tiles; the pillars in the station are the same colour. On the nearby road there is a lorry load of pigs all swaying from side to side with the motion of the open truck as we pass, rather like a synchronised dance group.

In and around Thung Song Junction

On the edge of town among all the lush greenery are a temple and a statue of Guan Yin, the Goddess of Mercy. Nearby, on a piece of rail and surrounded by lovely roses, is a steam locomotive; the only detail that I am able to get is its number – 277.

It is now ten to twelve and the train has reached Hat Yai. This is an important junction and is where most trains split, with part continuing to the Malaysian border about twenty minutes away while the other line continues along the east coast of Thailand. There is a fifteen-minute stop here and as always there is the opportunity to buy food from vendors on the platform, including spicy cooked chicken. I can see a lot of high-rise buildings which is not surprising as it is one of the biggest cities in Thailand and attracts a lot of visitors from nearby Malaysia. Like a lot a small towns and villages around the world, Hat Yai only started to develop and grow after the railway arrived.

Hot and spicy street food

As we get nearer to the border there is an absolute forest of rubber trees on both sides of the track, those fickle things that are often difficult to grow at home. Because the train is now running so late there is a change of plan and when we arrive at Pedang Besar on the Malaysian border we have to complete the customs formalities and transfer to a coach. The reason given is that the railway company are going to abandon the rest of the scheduled journey to Butterworth and return to Bangkok; by this ploy they should arrive back in Bangkok on time, but there is no mention of any passengers who might have wanted to join the train between here and Butterworth, or even those who might have wanted to join between Butterworth and here on the way back. There is an enormous amount of container traffic at Pedang Besar although I am not sure whether it is going to, or from, Thailand.

Pedang Besar

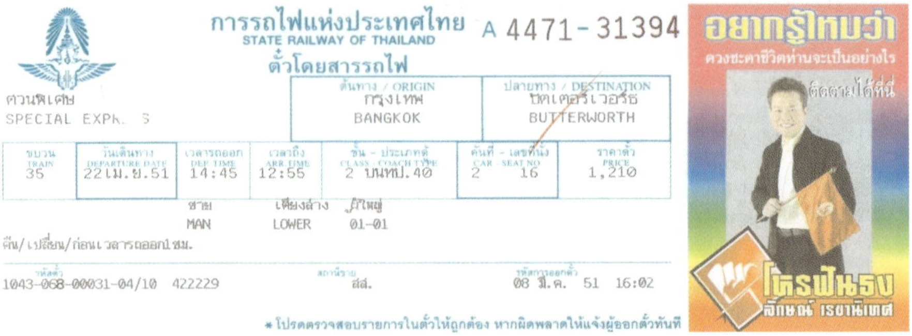

My Special Express ticket

The schedule is going to remain the same, except that the journey to Butterworth will be by coach and from there a transfer, again by coach, to the Holiday Inn on Penang Island for two nights. Arriving in Butterworth there is a quayside atmosphere, with many boats; there is also a big black steam locomotive on a plinth, 564.25 *Kuala Lumpur.*

Kuala Lumpur at Butterworth

Butterworth was named after William John Butterworth who was governor of the Straits Settlements from 1843 to 1855, but I am sure that he would not recognise it today for it is now a substantial container port. In the nineteenth century it was merely a landing place for the ferries from George Town, the capital of Penang across the water. Although the ferry still operates, the vast majority of traffic between the two points now crosses this part of the Strait of Malacca on an eight-mile bridge. Crossing it today there is an incredible amount of traffic going both ways and the road is also in the process of being widened.

The Holiday Inn is certainly pleasing to the eye as I arrive here for a two-night stay. There is a pretty fountain in the middle of a small garden at the front and then a reception area with beautiful marble tiles that are lovely and cool after the heat outside.

Hotel fountain

The hotel is situated right on the beach which is fringed by sweeping casuarina trees and pristine-looking sand. Apart from a young woman on a horse I have this part of the beach to myself. There is a restaurant with one side of the hotel, open to the inviting-looking swimming pool, and on the other is a delightful garden with sun loungers on immaculately manicured grass.

The beach at Penang

Sun terrace at the Holiday Inn, Penang

I have a very large room with what is described as a double double bed and the luxury of that after the upper bunk on the train is quite a contrast. Despite the heat I decide to go for a stroll and after about half a mile from the hotel I come across a little piece of history: an old Austin van is parked in among some bushes and under a very dilapidated-looking tin roof that looks as though it might come down around me at any time. There is no telling how long it has been here, it might be two days, it might be two years, but the owner has inscribed some history on the back: 'My name is Austin of England model A35 850cc. I was born in 1960, I'm very rare in Malaysia. My apology for being very slow. Please take care of me thank you.'

I am reluctant to go too far into the thick bushes for fear of what might be in there, and so cannot get a 'long shot' of the van.

Austin of England

Tomorrow there will be a coach trip around some of the sights of Penang but for rest of today I decide to lounge about and relax, particularly as my railway journeys around the world don't very often include hotels in a location like this one. If I had thought I was going to get an early night then clearly I am disappointed, for after dark the street outside the hotel comes alive with noise and stalls on each side on the road for as far as the eye can see; the stalls are all brightly lit and there is a buzzing atmosphere with crowds of people. I have an enjoyable time bargaining with one stallholder for a Malaysian football shirt; I do love bargaining and picked up some skill in it in Morocco. A stallholder who says he is from Sir Lanka tries to sell me a cricket pullover. I don't even remember saying that I was interested in it but he pursues me down the street, lowering the price as he goes. There are some money-changers in little shops, sitting behind their counters, and they remind me a little of Fagin. I am surprised at the widely differing rates that you can get.

* * *

Another day and I am up early but this time the weather is quite different: there are a lot of forbidding clouds and the odd spot of rain just promises more. Outside the hotel, the street is back to normal and there is no evidence at all of what was here last night, as if they had all melted away like snow in summer.

First stop today is a batik factory and to get to it there is a pleasant stroll through a little Malay village; at the side of the path there are some durian trees. Batik printing is a craft that has been practised for over two thousand years and involves designs and patterns drawn by hand on textiles. Coloured patterns are then applied using wax and dyes; most of the finished patterns seem to be either floral or butterflies. There is a showroom next door and although there are many beautiful things hanging there I am not tempted.

Batik textile printing

We cross the island and drive along the seafront towards George Town; there is a long line of high-rise buildings ahead that dominate everything. At a small lay-by next to the beach the coach pulls in for a short stop so that we can have a look at Fort Cornwallis, but it is not possible to go into the fort today.

The view from the lay-by

The fort was named after the Governor-General of Bengal, Charles Cornwallis and was completed in 1810 as a defence against pirates and the French. Amazingly, the fort has never featured in any battle and apart from occasionally housing troops it has always been an administrative centre, but looking up at the cannons on top of the high fort wall my interest is not lessened: some of the cannons date from the seventeenth century. Just outside the fort there is a magnificent tamarisk tree, which must be all of 70 feet high.

Fort Cornwallis

It is now raining which is a pity because it means we will have to see Chinatown mainly through the coach window. Chinatown covers a huge area but then it would I suppose, because there is a large Chinese population here. It is a place very much of old buildings with wooden shutters and there are also lots of very old shop-houses: we pass one that sells only toilets. The shame about the scenery is that Chinatown seems almost surrounded by high-rise buildings. One of these is the Komtar Tower, a very tall building flying a Union Jack; the tower is rather like a twelve-sided Rubik cube, it mostly houses government offices.

Chinatown

A pink pagoda

Lunch is at a very pleasant café and I have freshly grilled fish followed by chicken with onion bhaji, yoghurt and fresh bread. Back on the coach we pass a shop advertising all sorts of things that you can buy for your dog, including full grooming kits. The name of the shop is 'Dogs R Us'. Another shop, this time a convenience store, has its name above it in big letters, 'Oh Quick Stop'.

Less frivolous matters dominate now as we are heading for the Christian cemetery on Northam Road. This cemetery is no longer used and has some of the oldest graves on the island; it is however full of dark, gnarled trees and is rather forbidding – I would not like to walk round here at night. This cemetery is also very historic, for as well as being the last resting place of many famous Englishmen who came to this island it also contains the grave of Francis Light, who was the founder of Penang. He was born in Suffolk in 1740 but when he was about 25 he was living near Phuket and learning to speak many languages, including Malay. On behalf of the British East India Company he later leased the island of Penang from the Sultan of Kedah and he served as superintendent of the colony until his death from malaria in 1794.

The words on his grave are: Beneath this stone lie the remains of Francis Light Esq. who first established this island as a British settlement. Died 21st October 1794.

When in Penang it is worth visiting Khoo Kongsi in Cannon Square. This complex is made up of a clan house, opera stage, 24 heritage units and a large courtyard and is known as the Jewel of Penang. In the mid nineteenth century the Khoo clan migrated from China to Penang and although they involved themselves in local trades they formed a close-knit community. At the beginning of the twentieth century they bought a plot of land in the Weld Quay area and built the impressive building that now stands there in order to have not only a place of worship, but also somewhere where they could continue with their work on the genealogy of the clan.

Inside there are two rooms, one on each side, commemorating the lives of famous men of this clan who were both influential and highly educated. They include Bachelors of Art and Commerce, JPs, accountants, economists, electronics experts and scientists; their degrees were from all over world including Malaya, Scotland, Singapore, London, New Zealand and Melbourne. The whole place is a haven of peace and tranquillity. The intricacy and beauty of their work and the opera stage with its lush colour and decoration are quite dazzling. There is a complete wall depicting warriors mounted on creatures such as lions, and although the lion that I photograph does have a rather benign expression, most of them are very aggressive-looking.

Coming out of Khoo Kongsi, on the other side of the road, are some lovely old colonial houses with little walled front gardens which could be in England were it not for the intricate carving on the front doors. Unfortunately, today is very dull and wet and not the best for photographs.

Clan house, Khoo Kongsi

The opera stage

Warrior and lion

The final visit today is a trip on the Penang Hill funicular railway which was opened in 1923. The single carriage covers the one-and-a-quarter-mile trip in about half an hour and takes you to the summit terminal at over 2200 feet above sea level. It is very pleasant gliding silently upwards towards the cooler air as although the rain has stopped it is still cloudy and humid.

Penang Hill funicular railway

Getting off at the terminal, the first thing I see are monkeys running free, quite unafraid of the people walking about. A short walk up the path brings me to a café and a welcome ice cream. The view from up here is special and George Town, the Malacca Strait and Butterworth are all spread out below. Looking back down the way I can see that it is all thickly forested and standing here I can hear a lot of birds singing in the trees. In the distance I can see a thin line across the water, which is the eight-mile bridge.

Back at the bottom of the hill there are a lot of young people waiting to use the funicular railway; they are all smiles and are delighted to have their photograph taken.

What a view

A monkey trying to stare me out

Back at the hotel I decide to explore the little lanes that disappear into the trees from the road outside. The little dusty and narrow palm-fringed streets behind the main road of Batu Ferringhi seem to hold an air of mystery and the sounds from the main road are soon lost as I venture further. It is very quiet and peaceful, and as the street winds its

A school outing at Penang Hill

way through the trees I come across a small, thin cockerel scratching in the dust and a large white and brown cat dozing in the sun. Two small children are absorbed in a game with two sticks. Small houses with corrugated iron roofs nestle against palm trees; most of the houses have a small veranda and on one there is an old man fast asleep. Without thinking I tiptoe past.

It has been a long and interesting day and there is another one to look forward to tomorrow, although the journey will not be as planned because upgrading and alteration work to the rail line means that the rest of the journey to Kuala Lumpur will be by coach. There is an advantage to this arrangement, as there will be a stop to see the Perak Caves on the way and also a lunch opportunity in Ipoh.

After turning off the bridge from Penang we pass Devil's Island, which is just offshore; it used to be a prison but is now a resort and eco park. Here on the mainland great swathes of land are being reclaimed and there are a lot of industrial and science parks. As we leave the built-up area the view changes dramatically and all around there are thousands and thousands of palm oil trees. Also along this part of the coast are large areas of mangrove which are encouraged and protected as they form an effective barrier against soil erosion from the sea. There is a fine of 10,000 Malaysian ringgit (just over £2,000) for cutting down one of the mangrove trees. On the east coast, where there is no such protection, upwards of 150 feet of coastline have been lost to the sea.

The view now changes again and it is all forest-covered mountains. The road that we are travelling along has been hewn out of the mountains and everywhere there are channels, gutters and gullies to take the massive amount of water that falls during the rainy season; without these the road would almost certainly be washed away.

We travel through the Kinta Valley and are close to Ipoh, a town that was named after a tree with a poisonous sap. In the early twentieth century Ipoh was a boom town for the extraction of tin but this mostly came to an end by about 1980. It has also been known as the 'dead town' because of the numbers of people who moved away to Kuala Lumpur and Singapore after the collapse of tin mining, but I prefer one of its other nicknames, The Bougainvillea City. The old and new towns of Ipoh are split by the Kinta river. It is now quite a wealthy town, partly because of its history and now because of tourist income.

Entering the outskirts there is a lot of cleared land and a little further on there are rows and rows of new houses, but there are also quite a lot of closed and derelict shops. The town does however have some beautiful old buildings, and the commercial centre is obviously new and probably only built in the last ten years. Its beautiful buildings include the railway station that was first completed in 1917 and then later rebuilt; it is a very Moorish-looking building with domes and turrets and is known by the locals as the Taj Mahal of Ipoh. It has recently undergone much renovation following an electrification and double-tracking project. There is also the town hall, which is a glistening white building with many columns and a distinctly Grecian appearance. It is

Ipoh railway station

only a quick drive through the city, which is a pity. After lunch we are on the way to the caves at Perak.

Perak Cave Temple (Perak Tong) is situated at Jalan Kuala Kangsar, which is about three and a half miles from Ipoh, and is a very popular tourist attraction; as you approach you can see why. The ornate and beautiful frontage of the temple is built into the lushly covered limestone mountain and in front of it is a beautiful water garden.

Approaching Perak Tong

Perak Cave Temple

The water garden

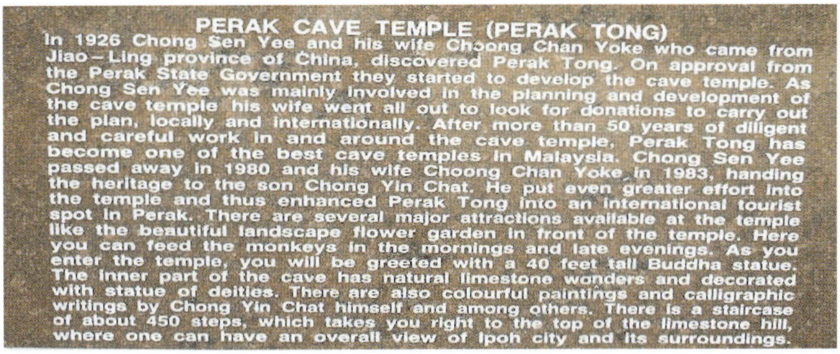

The story of Perak Tong

Inside the temple it is very quiet and dark, especially after the brightness outside. There are mystical murals on the walls and many Buddhas and other figures; there is also a very strong smell of joss sticks. The ceiling of the cave, for this is what it once was, is lost in darkness.

Inside Perak Cave Temple

Venturing into the back of the cave, past all the murals and figures, I find a staircase hewn out of the limestone that leads upwards to the top of the mountain. The plaque at the entrance says that it is 450 steps, and by the time I get to the top I can well believe it. The view is the reward as Ipoh is spread out below me, framed by the trees and the mountain.

Ipoh from the cave top

By the time I have negotiated the 450 steps back down I am just about ready to sink into my comfortable seat on the coach and think about Kuala Lumpur.

The view from the coach window on the journey to Kuala Lumpur is almost continuous forest-covered mountains; the trees that form that covering are an unbelievably rich green colour. Eventually, the view changes to a few scattered houses, then the outskirts of the city and now I can see the skyscrapers of the city proper.

Kuala Lumpur in Malay means 'muddy meeting place'. There are busy dual carriageways now and the road builders have kept pieces of natural jungle between carriageways and at the edge of the road. We are now in the city proper. My hotel is conveniently situated near a metro station and is also close to the centre of the city; the staff in reception are very welcoming and there are beautiful bouquets of flowers everywhere.

After figuring out that the lift will not operate without my room card, I eventually reach my room, which is on the seventh floor with a lovely view of the city with its many high-rise buildings, including the Petronas Towers. There are also a lot of large and beautiful trees and they are a striking contrast to the concrete and glass buildings.

After settling in at my hotel I set off to the old Kuala Lumpur station, part of which is now occupied by the Heritage Station Hotel, although everything about the old station has been preserved. The original integrated

The view from the hotel lift

and covered roadway at the front with its high domed ceiling is still here; this was so passengers could alight both in safety and under cover from inclement weather. This gleaming white building with its minarets, cupolas and Moorish arches was completed in 1911 and was constructed to the same specifications that were used for railway stations in England, although visually there is no comparison. The brilliant blue of the sky makes a perfect backdrop for this very striking and attractive building, which was replaced as the city's main rail terminal in 2001 by the new KL Central Station a few streets away, although commuter and freight trains still pass through the perfectly preserved platforms of the old station.

Walking through the front door I see that the original beautifully wood-panelled booking office counter is now the hotel reception, and the booking hall, a comfortable place for refreshment. There is just one couple having a cup of tea and a sandwich here, sitting on plush green high-back upholstered chairs.

Passing through a door I find myself on the platform of what still looks like a working station, although passengers no longer use it as they now have to embark on their journey from the new station some distance away. There are many platforms and tracks and in front of me is a stationary cement train; it is like a ghost station, as everything is in place except that there are no passengers. Over the entire station there

Kuala Lumpur old station, now the Heritage Station Hotel

is a beautifully preserved cast iron and glass roof. The platforms are beautifully tiled and there are fresh flowers growing in containers.

Standing on the buffers of the cement train to take a photograph I am jolted out of my reverie by the sound of clanking buffers, and I just have time to leap from the train before it moves away. Between two platforms on the far side a commuter train suddenly glides silently by, as though it does not want to disturb the tranquillity of this place.

A passenger-free zone

Not far from the station and still in the heart of this big and bustling modern city is a lovely swathe of grass; it is the former cricket ground from colonial days complete with club house and the Spotted Dog pub, although it is now called the Royal Selangor Club and is exclusive to the city's elite. The original building, which was built in 1884, was the centre of colonial life and also where expatriates could watch cricket. The building was destroyed by fire in 1970 and the black and white mock Tudor building of today that was built in 1980 is a reproduction of the old club.

The club is an anachronism, standing in the shadow of a brand new skyscraper, but somehow this cricket ground and other relics of the past like the railway station, have a different beauty and the old and the modern complement each other. Many of the old British colonial houses and offices have also been preserved.

The Royal Selangor Club

Calling back at the hotel to pick up some camera batteries I see that a notice has appeared outside my hotel bedroom on the seventh floor, with the heading Routine Pesticide Control. It says, 'The hotel will conduct a routine pesticide control this week encompassing the internal areas of the hotel, please note that the odour, because of the chemical application, may cause slight discomfort or irritation, however the odour will dissipate within the hour. You may also find some of the cockroaches coming out of their hideouts due to the chemical reactions after the exercise.'

The city centre is surrounded and linked by a rail system that is very efficient, clean and inexpensive, and I am going to use it for my next visit, which is to the Petronas Towers. These towering twin peaks are linked by a walkway halfway up and are still the highest linked towers in the world.

At the station close to my hotel the first train that I take is an underground one, which passes through tunnels that are brightly lit and clean. The platforms are all guarded, and as the train comes in and stops, its doors are in line with corresponding lines on the platform.

On the same station I climb a flight of stairs to catch a linked service, only this is above ground. Then it is another change, this time to a monorail which glides silently between the gleaming skyscrapers, houses, markets and the river; the view of the city from the monorail is really special.

The view from the monorail

The monorail glides silently into the terminal of the line. Looking at the sign at the end of the platform I just have to turn round. The sign reads, DEAD turn back and look.

Monorail terminal and sign

From here it is a short walk to the Petronas Towers. Standing at the bottom and looking up at this great edifice of glass and stainless steel I get a feeling that is a bit like vertigo in reverse. These towers, which were completed in 1998, are 1483 feet high with 88 storeys and were

The Petronas Towers with sky bridge

named after Petronas, the national petroleum and oil company. The sky bridge linking the towers is on the 41st floor and there is a queue each day for the limited free tickets that are issued to use it. The sun sparkles and reflects from this very impressive building and it is quite dazzling; it is also very hot standing outside, and it is good get inside.

The offices of many of the city's well-known and affluent businesses are in the towers but it is also a place to shop, and what a place! Inside the towers and spread over six floors is Suria KLCC, one of the busiest and glitziest shopping malls in the city and my first impression of a vast shopping centre. Here you can buy anything you want, which certainly looks to be true as all the international department stores appear to be here along with specialist outlets, banks, coffee bars and chain stores; there is even a cinema.

On the ground floor far below there is a children's fashion show in progress; it is for 10- to 12-year-olds and appears to be a very professionally produced event. There is a huge crowd of people watching it.

Level two is one enormous food hall with a multitude of selling outlets and hundreds of people sitting at tables eating. I get the impression that

Suria shopping mall

Fashion show

you could buy almost anything you like to eat here although it seems a bit expensive. Walking past a table I can see a man on his own eating a curry with an air of urgency; perhaps he is late for work. I'm not sure but I think it may have been beef and potato massaman, one of my favourite curries. At another table there is a group of people who are obviously English tourists; they are trying, without much success, to get two young children of about 9 or 10 to eat noodles; the children have spotted a Macdonalds across the hall and are demanding a burger. Looking through a window I can see sparkling water and lush gardens outside and it suddenly seems a better option than the multitude of people in here.

The view from the Petronas Towers

Stepping outside onto the forecourt I realise I have forgotten how hot it is outside, but the sound of tinkling fountains and the shade of the many trees is very relaxing. The gardens surrounding the lake are very lush and make a wonderful island of green in this skyscraper city. Although not really a city person, today I have found the complementing old and the new of Kuala Lumpur to be both interesting and attractive, and it seems a shame that I am only here for three days.

The walk back to the hotel is not a long one, but as I sit at an outside café on the way back, sipping an ice cold lime and lemonade, I am reminded of an old black and white film starring John Mills: *Ice Cold in Alex.*

Another day and this time I am heading for the Central Market for a different and more pleasurable shopping experience. I do like shopping, particularly when I go abroad as you always find different and more interesting things. I take the monorail again, this time to central station and then a walk across to central station mainline which is just like a huge airport terminal with different lines on different levels. It is a bit of a daunting place when you see it for the first time but I soon find the overhead light rail system and that takes me smoothly to a station from where it is a pleasant walk alongside the river to Kuala Lumpur Central Market.

The market is in an old 1930s Art Deco building that used to be the fresh produce market until it fell into disuse and disrepair. It was reopened in the 1980s as a modern shopping complex although as you walk round it has a very much traditional feel and atmosphere. What a fantastic shopping place this is: arts and crafts, clocks, pottery, paintings, batik, clothes and wood carvings. There are restaurants on the ground and first floors and you can have anything from a can of lemonade to various Malaysian dishes; I didn't see chips in any of them – what a nice change.

I do like clocks

The market is very busy and there are many lovely things to buy, none of those types of things that are generally reserved for the tourist market. On an upstairs floor I get into conversation with Efe (pronounced eevar); she is twenty years old and a delightfully cheerful young girl. She is also in charge of a stall selling beautiful dresses and scarves of every imaginable colour and style, also ties in brilliant shades of colour. I settle for a bright yellow one with a bright red slash across it. Efe's face creases in smiles as I manage to get her to pose for a photograph holding my purchase.

We have a conversation about where I have come from and where I have been; Bangkok she knows but not Chiang Mai. She giggles a lot, especially when she realises that I have my pocket dictaphone on. She tells me that she has a little dog and he is nine months old; she is also intrigued by my grey hair and we have a little guessing game about how old we think the other is.

Efe is very keen to be assured that I am well, and I in turn ask the same of her. After three mutual enquiries on this subject we part as good friends, her final comment being, 'You very young.' This would be good for my ego except that she is giggling. It is yet another delightful cultural exchange and the fact that we are of a different sex, a different age and from different countries means nothing. Each of us has had pleasure from the meeting and certainly for me, and I hope for her also, there is a nice memory to take away.

A short walk brings me to Merdeka Square and on the side of a busy road is a mosque-type building with a very tall clock tower. This is the Sultan Abdul Samad Building; it was erected in 1897 for use as the headquarters of the colonial administration and was named after the ruler of Selangor at the time.

It has elegant arched windows and cupolas and has remained unchanged while the city around it has modernised. The impressive-looking clock tower is over 140 feet high, including the large dome, which was originally made of copper sheets laid over timber beams. Although the building was originally built for the State Secretary's department and other government offices, it now houses the Federal Court, the Appeals Court and the High Court.

The Sultan Abdul Samad Building

Looking from Sultan Abdul Samad building

* * *

I don't really consider myself a city person, but after exploring this very interesting city over the last two days, with its mix of old, new and colonial buildings and its very friendly people, there is a definite tinge of sadness about leaving. It would be good to come back here again.

It has been a long journey since that breakfast of beef and potato mussaman curry in Chiang Mai. I have been very fortunate to see some wonderful things and places, and to meet some really nice people along

Efe, a happy Malaysian

the way. If I had to pick out three very special memories they would be riding elephants, eating durian fruit and, best of all, meeting Efe.

PART II

Morocco

On my journeys through different countries I always try to combine train travel with meeting people from different cultures, so with a fairly comprehensive rail system and a population whose way of life has not changed in hundreds of years, Morocco was a natural choice.

I start this journey as I mean to continue in Morocco, by train. As we approach Crewe station I can see the lovely steam locomotive Princess Elizabeth 6201 in the Heritage Centre siding; she looks very smart in her maroon livery. The Duchess of Sutherland, also in maroon, is there as well, together with the old Advanced Passenger Train, a neglected reminder of the early days of tilting trains in the UK.

The Airbus 319 takes off on time from Manchester airport for the short hop to Heathrow. A fitful sun is trying to break through the clouds and as the aeroplane climbs I can see the huge Jodrell Bank telescope far below, but from up here it looks like a tiny toy. As we reach cruising height there is a carpet of cloud stretching away to the horizon; it looks like thousands of large cotton wool balls. Dropping through the clouds to Heathrow I can clearly see the Millennium Dome beneath me, the first time that I have seen it.

The Millennium Dome from the air

At Heathrow I get into conversation with Ben, who lives in London but was born in Malaysia, and we soon have a conversation going about Kuala Lumpur, a city that I visited following my trip to Thailand. We talk about its cleanliness, amazing transport system, incredible shopping facilities and places that we both know there. He is also going to Morocco and is going to stay in a rhiad in Marrakech with his girlfriend; she tells me her name is Rachel and she is following along behind Ben. They are full of excitement at their forthcoming trip.

Although Morocco has been much influenced by Europe it is still an exotic land with an air of mystery and excitement. My itinerary includes most of the major cities followed by a visit to the Todra Gorge and a trek into the Sahara. Like Ben and Rachel I am looking forward to this trip, and board my flight to Casablanca with a keen sense of anticipation.

I arrive in Casablanca in the evening of a beautiful night with a full moon and a relaxing temperature of 75 degrees Fahrenheit. The drive to my hotel will only take about 30 minutes and is along what seems to be an endless dual carriageway with palm trees down the centre. The driver's radio is playing local music, which I find both relaxing and stimulating, and by the time that I reach the hotel I am starting to feel at home in this exotic and exciting land.

Morocco is a place of contrasts: fashionable hotels and restaurants exist side by side with centuries-old markets or historic fortified districts. The medieval bazaars have existed in their present form for hundreds of years and are mostly populated by people in traditional dress going about their business in the same way as it has always been done, while in the bigger cities the cars, skyscrapers and besuited pedestrians could be from any big city in the world. There are also extremes of weather: in the winter there is heavy snow on the Atlas Mountains while oranges are ripening in the northern lowlands and hot sun is blazing down on the southern sand dunes.

It is 10.15 pm and from the window of my room I can see a swimming pool below with some birds drinking at the edge. In the middle of blocks of houses I can see a beautiful minaret lit up by searchlights that accentuate the gleaming blue, white and brown mosaic work and the white dome with a finial on the top. The combination of flying, driving with music and a superb dinner of beef Moroccan style with black olives has rendered me ready for bed but adrenalin is keeping me awake. At 11.30 pm, although it is obviously now very dark, I can see the clouds white against a very dark-blue sky and all the buildings are gleaming white in the darkness.

I am up at 6.30 am. It is Sunday and the hotel is very quiet, as are the streets outside, and as I stand on the shining marble of the hotel foyer and study the intricate marblework of the pavements outside I can see from the brazen sky that there is a hot day ahead. This morning will mainly be taken up by a visit to the Hassan II Mosque, followed by a train to Fez at 12.15 pm.

There is a pleasant drive along a palm-tree-lined avenue past the port area to the mosque. Outside it there is a vast courtyard that is already filling up with tourists and others who have come to see this majestic structure, which is awesome in scale both inside and out. Some idea of its scale is in its capacity, which is 80,000 people; there is also a subterranean car park with spaces for 1100 cars and forty coaches.

The Hassan II Mosque

The minaret is two hundred metres high and towers over Casablanca. The whole scene is set against a brilliant blue sky and the aquamarine waters of the sea, and looking up I can see a kestrel chasing the pigeons that seem to be nesting in the apertures of the mosaic. The coolness inside is very welcome and I stand looking down the immensely long hall of the Oratory, lined on both sides with beautiful marble columns and lit by many chandeliers which sparkle and reflect off the gleaming marble floor; the capacity of this hall is a staggering 25,000 people.

On each side and the full length of this beautiful hall there are raised areas intricately crafted from wood and some fifteen feet above the floor; the capacity of these areas is 5000, and they are where the women make their prayers. High above me is a very beautiful and ornate ceiling made of cedarwood from the south of Morocco; I am surprised to learn that this vast ceiling can open to the sky in four minutes.

We go downstairs, and underneath the mosque is the vast ablution room with what looks like a huge array of toadstools that the water comes out of. There is a strict religious ritual to washing before you pray which includes washing your hands three times, together with your ears and your feet.

The artistic grandeur of the mosque both inside and out seems to me to be a justification for the ten thousand craftsmen who worked on

The ablution room, with our guide Zahir

its construction. Everywhere there is ornate mosaic work and beautiful marble. All the construction materials were of Moroccan origin except the many chandeliers, which came from Venice. After the death of King Mohammed V in 1961, his son King Hassan II considered building a mausoleum for his father in Casablanca but then decided to build it in Rabat instead. Because of his change of heart over the location of his father's tomb, King Hassan II felt that he owed a debt to the people of Casablanca and the construction of the mosque was by way of payment of that debt. It was built between 1987 and 1993, and covers an area of 9 hectares of which 6 hectares stand on the sea bed: this gives it the appearance of rising out of the waters of the Atlantic. Although it is protected from the sea by an ornate sea wall I can see that construction work is ongoing in reclamation work alongside the mosque.

It is now time to go and we drive alongside the Atlantic. There is a nice beach with a succession of private and public sections together with

Sea view from the Hassan Tower

private and public swimming pools. There are also several cafés and even a well-known fast food outlet. Our guide Zahir says that it is over 80°F today but too cold for swimming; he says that only non-Moroccan people will be swimming today.

On the other side of the road there is another of Morocco's contrasts. We have just passed what looks like a very poor shanty town that is completely surrounded by a 12-foot wall with pink oleanders growing all along it. This is followed almost immediately by a tidy residential park with palm trees and immaculately clipped lawns, and then a very smart palace that used to belong to the Saudi royal family. This part of Casablanca is known as the Corniche and it is a very select area; there are palm trees and greenery everywhere, together with more pink oleanders and other bright flowers.

On the seaward side of the Corniche there is tremendous development going on, with many hotels and restaurants springing up, and nearly everywhere there are newly planted avenues of fully grown palm trees. It is part of Morocco's bid to woo more tourists. There is time for a coffee before leaving for the train, and this at a very nice restaurant fronting the sea. There is quite a wind blowing and the white horses of the sea are charging the rocky coast. The staff are very friendly and welcoming, and let me onto the roof area to take a photograph of this exhilarating view. Walking back to the coach for the journey to the station I see a jacaranda tree in full bloom.

The view from the restaurant

The roads here are excellent and are lined with 30-foot yucca trees, their great bunches of white flowers stirring in what is now a gentle breeze from the sea. There is a profusion of bougainvillea in different colours and the tall hedges are clipped oleander bushes. We pass a large building, and outside on the pavement there are two workmen on their knees laying small pieces of mosaic into the pathway. Each piece is about three inches by one inch.

We pass the old medina where there is a café with a long row of men sitting outside drinking coffee, reading newspapers and relaxing in the sun – very nice. The business part of the city is very modern looking and not unlike other cities of the world. There is a brief stop on the Boulevard de la Resistance where our guide leaves us before the last leg to Casablanca rail station. It is a chance to stretch legs and say goodbyes, but I am immediately surrounded by water sellers. The guerrab (water seller) is now a less common sight in places like Casablanca but they can still be found plying their trade in the medinas of places like Fez and Marrakech. These gentlemen see this as tourist opportunity and although they are in full costume, their leather water carriers are empty and their trade today is more mercenary.

The water sellers

Having got through to them that I do not wish to purchase watches, gold rings, necklaces or other items of personal jewellery, I then agree a fee for taking photographs. They are dressed in scarlet djellabas, and each has a broad-brimmed, tasselled and multi-coloured hat with a string of brass bowls and cups around his neck. Although most of them are wearing sandals, one of them spoils the picture slightly with designer trainers. The outfit is completed with a small brass bell on a chain with which to attract customers. Eventually, everyone is satisfied with either money or photographs, and we part with smiles and handshakes.

Casablanca railway station is a surprise for me. I had expected a rather run down and inefficient railway system, and the sight of spotlessly clean and beautifully tiled floors and walls everywhere, together with many

Casablanca station

Casablanca main platform

Tidy tracks at Casablanca station

potted palms, is a very pleasing one. Even the track bed between the platforms is devoid of any type of litter or rubbish.

The station hall with its great domed ceiling and chandeliers is thronged with people, many in traditional clothes although there is a sprinkling of men in suits. A man with a white skull cap and long flowing green djellaba strides past. A woman of indeterminate age walks past me without a glance, struggling with a very large bag; she is clothed from head to toe in black with only a tiny slit for her eyes. She is followed by a young Moroccan woman of about eighteen or nineteen who is dressed in very tight jeans, a skimpy, low-cut top and black boots. Yet another example of Morocco's tolerant contrasts.

Outside there are many petite taxis plying their trade between the building and a line of mature fig trees. The station is very hot and busy; the booking hall is thronged with people and it appears that the train is running late although no one seems to know by how much. It seems a long time since my morning coffee so I head for the station café, where I am treated to a cup of strong sweet Moroccan coffee by the two people running this establishment. I am the first westerner that they have served today and it is very easy to start a conversation with them. They are very interested to know about England and why I have come to Morocco; it is a great opportunity to learn a few more words of Moroccan Arabic.

New friends at Casablanca station

I had also expected ageing diesel locomotives with perhaps the odd steam loco, but the entire Moroccan rail system is electrified. The gleaming red and yellow Hitachi electric locomotive pulling in its twelve coaches is yet another surprise in this country of surprises. They have also recently introduced very smart double-decker trains and there is one in the siding.

The new double-decker train

We expect to arrive in Fez at 4.30 pm, a journey of about four and quarter hours. We pass several stations without stopping; all with the same beautiful tiled platforms with many trees and flowers. All the stations have extensive sidings and it is already obvious that the railway competes better than very well for the haulage of both passengers and freight. It is no wonder that this train is very busy for in speed and efficiency it cannot be matched by road, I am sure: we must be doing at least 100 mph.

Railway platforms are beautifully planted

Although we are currently hurtling along between a seemingly never-ending avenue of eucalyptus trees, the view from the train has been quite varied. A large construction site with massive drain pipes exposed the dark sandstone red of the soil where the surface had been ripped away; then an open-air market along the railside, followed by what I can only describe as a garden centre *exotique* with fantastic-shaped carvings and statues, the whole place covered with purple, yellow and red bougainvilleas. We also saw an enormous timber-processing factory which even at this speed took us several minutes to pass by. The refreshment trolley on this train is excellent and the café noir, mint tea and sandwiches have been very good.

About an hour's journey time from Fez we run into a more mountainous area and there is huge expanse of sugar cane with dozens of white egrets standing silently around. We pass a man on a donkey herding goats and sheep, and in trying to describe the sight my notes say 'more man than donkey.' There are now many olive groves dotted around the hillsides with the mountains in the background. We leave Sidi Kacem where the line continues north to Tangier, while we turn east to Meknes and Fez.

The view outside is now of a seemingly unending vista of olive trees. Walking down the corridor of the rocking train I come across a man at the end of the carriage smoking a cigarette; he has rather guilty air as though he should not be there. I get into conversation with him and find out that his name is Mohammed and he works in the building trade. He says he earns about 100 dirhams a day (about £8) and that the bosses earn much more than him.

Nearing Meknes there are a lot of grapevines to be seen, but I have yet to taste Moroccan wine. From a rail map of Morocco on the carriage wall I discern the following as being the rail system of Morocco, although I discover later that there is building programme under way in which new lines will connect as yet unconnected places: Marrakech to Casablanca to Rabat to

Kenitra to Sid Kacem and then north to Tangier. From Sidi Kacem the line goes east to Meknes to Fez to Oujda on the Algerian border and then into Algeria itself. From Oujda there is a line south to Bouarfa near the Algerian border. From Benguerir (north of Marrakech) there is a line west to Safi on the coast, and from Casablanca there is a line south to El Jadida, also on the coast. Just south of Casablanca there is a line as far as Khouribga and Oued Zem, although from looking at an old map of Morocco it seems that this line once continued east to Kasba Tadla and then north to Fez.

The line is curving more now that we are in the mountains and everywhere looks very brown and hot and dry; even the crops look tired. It is 3.30 pm and we are running into the outskirts of Meknes. There are a lot of tent dwellers alongside the railway, together with tin shacks that have their roofs held down with tyres. Meknes station is another very clean and smart place with mosaic work floors and platforms.

Meknes station

We arrive at Fez station. Walking down the platform between two trains I see a long line of orange trees laden with fruit. At a station on the way I had taken the opportunity to hop out of the train and pick one of these

Orange tree at Fez station

fruits, but although nicely coloured and ripe it was incredibly tart and I am not tempted to try them again here.

Inside and outside the Royal Mirage Hotel

It is ten to five and there is just a short transfer to the Royal Mirage Hotel; plenty of time for a wash and brush up before dinner. My room is large and very nice, with two double beds, gleaming bathroom, walk-in wardrobes, armchairs and a balcony that overlooks the swimming pool.

In the evening a group of us go out to a folklore show: Andalusian music together with Berber music and an acrobatic musical team in full traditional costume. This is followed by a magician who makes things appear and disappear, after which there is a belly dancer who concludes her act with a display of fire eating. The final performance is a re-enactment of a traditional Moroccan wedding, and I am extremely surprised to find that I have been selected to play the part of the groom, with Zahir on hand to steady my 'pre-wedding nerves'. Two attendants dress me in a white djellaba and gold headdress, while my 'bride' is dressed in a very sumptuous outfit with lots of coloured sequins. The

Berber musicians

bride and her attendants are then ritually displayed to the audience, followed by the holding of hands and dancing together. It proves to be a very enjoyable and interesting evening! I find out later that the King of Morocco has forbidden the practice of men having more than one wife, although there is a concession that it is permitted if the first wife agrees.

The belly dancer and fire eater

Bride, groom and retinue!

I am up at 6.30 am. Already it is a glorious hot day, which will be taken up exploring the old city of Fez with its centuries-old medina. The population of Fez is approximately one million, of which two hundred thousand live in the old medina.

Before we get to the medina we make a short stop to visit a local factory producing pottery ware; outside there is a large pile of raw grey pottery and ornaments drying in the sun. There is also an enormous pile of olive pips, and I learn that they are used in the furnaces as they produce a very high heat when they burn and are ideal for the firing process. It is good that a waste product from olives is such an essential ingredient in the manufacture of these clay items.

In what looks like to me a dark, small and hot sweatshop a young man is kneading the grey clay to make it more pliable; next to him another man is effortlessly producing vases and bowls on his spinning pottery wheel – he makes it look so easy! In another room a young man on his own is painstakingly laying out a pattern of small mosaic pieces on the floor for what looks like a table top.

Kneading the clay

Laying out a mosaic

Next, there is an underground room without windows and lit by fluorescent tubes. It is incredibly hot, even though there are fans humming. There are about fifteen men and women in here engaged in decorating bowls and ornaments, and their skill is a treat to watch as they paint tiny intricate lines and patterns all by hand and transform a plain blank into a thing of beauty.

Outside in a covered yard there are a group of men engaged in cutting and shaping small pieces of mosaic for fixing to the pottery ware. It is

Hand decorating a pot

an extremely dirty job: the men squat on the dry earthen floor that is mixed with grey clay dust, and as they sweat the dust clings to them till they all look like grey gnomes. In the shop, and looking at the beautiful things on sale, it is difficult to reconcile them with the conditions under which they were produced. Everything is very expensive, and I speculate on how much of the individual price of each item went to the workers who produced it. Outside there is a beautiful view of the hills beyond Fez.

The view from the pottery shop

We have another short stop to see Dar el-Makhzen (the royal palace), the oldest palace in Morocco. Its two-hundred-acre site is surrounded by a huge brown wall. When I attempt to take a photograph of a side gate with guards on either side they wave me away furiously, but follow that with smiles when I acknowledge their gestures with an apology. I learn later that it was a service gate and it is forbidden to photograph any palace goods being either delivered or collected.

Before we enter Fez medina we are driven to the top of a hill for an aerial view. The old medina is in a valley surrounded by mountains and

Entrance to the royal palace

its perimeter wall that is twelve centuries old is made from lime, stones and sand (no cement). Along its twelve-kilometre length much of the battlements and watch towers are still intact. Inside the perimeter wall the square houses are packed together, and from my viewpoint it is like looking at a sea of beige and cream blocks. The view is quite spectacular and it is only from up here that you can really appreciate the packed sprawl that seems to stretch from one end of the valley to another.

The old medina at Fez

Although the ground looks brown and dry, outside the medina there is a large olive grove. Although they must need water, every time I see olive groves they always seem to be in an area of great dryness. High on the top of another hill I can see a sixteenth-century military fort that is still in use; flags are flying from the battlements and I can just see some figures, looking like ants from this distance.

Driving outside the old walls this place is buzzing with people and is full of life and activity; there are mules everywhere and nearly everyone is in national dress. The sense of movement, colour and noise is almost overwhelming.

The medina gate

Inside the medina the buildings are jammed together so tightly that there is no room for any vehicles and everything has to go on foot or by mule. The streets are covered at the top with wickerwork to keep the sun out and are crowded together with shops on both sides selling all manner of things, including spices, dates, clothes, glass, chandeliers, fruit, kitchenware, lamps, carpets, fried eggs, hot pancakes, grandfather clocks, nuts, gorgeous sticky sweet things, meat, brass ornaments, musical instruments, silverware, leather jackets, hats, scarves, pointed shoes; the list could go on.

In the old medina

In a small square there is a big tree, and under its spreading branches there are several men beating copper and making dozens of utensils and bowls; there is also a small café with men outside drinking coffee and mint tea. A man on a donkey comes past loaded with a box of live rabbits. I stoop to stroke a tiny little black and white kitten with the most enormous ears, and immediately a young boy aged six or seven rushes over, smiles at me and says, 'Two thousand euros?'

Some of the streets have craftsmen in them, such as carpenters, dyers, butchers, tanners, etc. There is even a street where only sewing machines are sold. There is an almost constant stream of mules carrying goods, and in the very narrow streets you have no warning of their approach. I have a bruised foot for a couple of days after it felt the weight of a fully laden mule.

A tight squeeze

The guide says that he has something special to show me, and we enter a small shop that is full from floor to ceiling with the ubiquitous pointy-toed slippers. I am looking at a bright yellow pair and thinking what will I do with them when I get home when he urges me on up a narrow flight of stairs. At the top there is a balcony. Spread before me is a wonderful view of old Fez, but my attention is drawn to the sight below. It is like a giant stone honeycomb of seventy or so vats, each about four or five feet across, each one filled with a coloured liquid. The different colours, red, saffron yellow, blue, green, brown, white and pink, give it the appearance of huge paintbox. It is a perfectly preserved mediaeval tannery, and the guide tells me that hundreds of years ago there would have been two hundred of these in Fez. A giant wheel raises water from the river and distributes it among the vats. The tanners add the hides and dye and then tread the mixture until the hide is thoroughly soaked. There is a very pungent smell rising up from below and this, with the heat of the sun, must make it one of the most tiring jobs imaginable. Not surprisingly I can see only young men below.

The tannery

Fez from the tannery

We move on to a tour of the old Jewish quarter, although Jews no longer live in this part. We also visit a very well-preserved seventeenth-century synagogue. This place is mass of little alleys, some of them cobbled.

The start of the Jewish quarter

We are in an area where there are lots of dentists. The guide says that some of them do not charge much money but there is no guarantee of their work; as I look down a narrow alleyway into a small courtyard, I can see a man with what looks like a pair of pliers in his hand pulling a tooth from the mouth of a man in a small chair. Two other men are seated nearby, one of them cradling his jaw in his hand.

Down another aromatic alley there is a small wool factory where I learn that wool from live sheep is used for weaving, while wool from dead sheep is used for stuffing cushions.

'Live' wool at the front, 'dead' wool at the back

There are many, many small shops in this quarter and it is very noticeable that in most of them the proprietor has a long duster that he uses on whatever he has displayed for sale. All the bags, fabrics etc. look very clean, which is remarkable in this hot and dusty atmosphere. Down another small alley, through a very dark opening and down two or three steps, I can make out two young men bent over sewing machines, surrounded by mounds of what looks like silk. Although outside it is a brilliantly sunny day, down there they have small lights over their machines.

Back in the hotel I reflect on the day and write up my notes. The kaleidoscope of sights and sounds has been both tiring and invigorating, and I look forward to another day tomorrow.

Another bright and hot morning. Today is a drive to the Roman city of Volubilis and then the holy city of Moulay Idris. It is a long straight drive on a smooth tarmac road, and for mile after mile there are olive groves on one side of the road and dry-looking agricultural land on the other. There is a temptation to nod off until suddenly the ride becomes very bumpy. I think at first it has become a dirt road, until I realise that there has been so much traffic from the people working the land on each side that the tarmac has become coated with a thick layer of packed dirt and stones. Incredibly, a little further on there is a lorry full of tarmac with men busy laying it over the dirt and stones.

The view changes. The land now suddenly looks very fertile, with a lot of wheat and vegetable crops. It seems that pesticides are not generally used in Morocco and this is obviously why from the coach window I can see swathes of wheat with beautiful red poppies and yellow daisies growing amongst it. Land is not wasted here, as in between the rows of olive trees wheat has been planted and the waving rows of gold between the dark green of the olives is very picturesque.

The land here is obviously rich as it is all cultivated. We pass a man standing with his legs apart and arms akimbo while he supervises four cows leisurely munching at the roadside. A little further on there is a man in a brown djellaba fast asleep in the middle of a field of broad beans. The occasional house that we pass is usually fairly substantial and painted in cream and pink. We descend a long road round the side of a deep and green valley and climb up the other side through the mountains; the view back is of a vast undulating plain of green and gold. During the previous autumn this area had more rain than in the last thirty years and this explains the lush crops and greenness.

We make a brief stop in what looks like the middle of nowhere, although it does have a name: Sidi Ched. From here there is wonderful view of a vast reservoir, with the tranquil blue of the water stretching to the mountains shimmering in the heat in the distance.

The reservoir

Ever since we left Fez an hour ago the heat has been relentless and the land so dry looking, and yet virtually all of it is under some sort of cultivation. At the side of the road there is a rough and ready tent built out of an old tarpaulin, and in a basket at the side some tired pieces of fruit are for sale. There is also a framework of posts attached to the tent and dangling from this there are several plastic bottles of different shapes and colours. As they are all empty it is difficult to see what purpose they have, although I later discover that they are for filling with olive oil to sell to passers-by. Despite the makeshift construction there are some animals about, and other indications that the man in the tent lives in this bleak and inhospitable spot on at least a semi-permanent basis.

Roadside olive oil shop

We now enter a small town, and although I can't see a name I think it is Nzala-des-Beni-Ammar. On the outskirts there are disused half-built houses side by side with very elegant constructions, and in the heart of this quite busy little town there are cafés with people drinking coffee, a small mosque, a post office and a market with a lot of donkeys tethered nearby. The main items for sale appear to be fruit and shoes.

It is very hilly country around here, a patchwork of colours: gold, dark brown, light brown, white, black and green. The road has been climbing higher and higher and as I look back at the sweep of mountains with their variety of colours below us I not only admire the savage beauty of the view but also think what an excellent oil painting it would make. The olive trees are now few and far between but suddenly there is one close by, and although there is no sign of human habitation as far as the eye can see, this solitary tree has a circle of men sitting around it, rather like an Indian pow-wow.

We turn off this road and are nearly at Volubilis. Around us the soil is very thin and poor with many stones showing through; however it is good ground for the prickly pear cactus and there are acres and acres of it, all heavy with fruit. We round a bend on the top of a hill and below us about a mile away is Volubilis. It was built on a slight mound in the middle of a vast plain, and we stop here for a few minutes to drink in the view and take photographs.

On the road to Volubilis

Volubilis from the road

Volubilis dates back to the Kings of Mauretania but reached its height of importance under the Romans in the second and third centuries when it was a major trading city. The Romans abandoned Volubilis in the early fifth century and although people continued to live here for another thirteen centuries, it was mostly a ruin throughout that time. During the eighteenth century it was discovered as a source of pre-cut marble and most of the buildings were pulled down to use the stone in the construction of Meknes.

Volubilis main street

The Triumphal Arch

It is incredibly hot today and I am reluctant to tear myself away from the ice cream vendor and the shade of the few trees at the entrance, but the site guide has no intention of leaving anyone behind; perhaps it means fewer tips if he does. From the entrance the site is roughly the shape of an upside-down letter L with the once main street (Via Decumanua Maximus) running through the entire length from the Tangier Gate to the Triumphal Arch, a sandstone structure built to honour the Emperor Caracalla in AD 217.

Most of the important buildings were along this colonnaded street and there are some beautifully preserved mosaic floors in a lot of them,

I've seen it all before

especially the House of Ephebus with its mosaic of Bacchus, the god of wine and the House of Orpheus with scenes from classical mythology. In the House of Venus there are also some lovely mosaics including Perseus and the Gorgon. Looking to the left of the arch is the site of the House of the Dog, which our guide says was a brothel: indeed there is a large stone phallus adjacent to it.

Mosaics at Volubilis

Despite the eighteenth-century destruction, the colonnades of the Basilica (Public Hall) still stand and are impressive. There are also many other things to see including the Temple of Saturn, the Public Baths, the oil presses and the Capitol building.

On top of a tall column just past the Basilica storks have built a huge nest, so huge in fact that several sparrows are using it as a nesting site as well. Another stork arrives and regurgitates food for their young, although I cannot see them; this is then followed by one of the adults producing a loud noise by rattling the two parts of its beak together.

It is incredibly peaceful here, looking at the olive-tree-dotted mountains all around, but I am beginning to wilt slightly after an hour under the fierce heat of the sun and recommend a hat to anyone wishing to visit

The Basilica colonnade

Storks nest on the top of a Roman column

this site. I take a short cut down from the Basilica into a dip with a small stream gurgling at the bottom. The sound of birds singing in the olive trees is very pronounced in this little valley.

Back at the tiny café under the trees I get into conversation with Reda, who is from Fez. He does not look more than about thirty-five years old, but says that he married an American girl and lived in Connecticut before getting divorced. He then married an Austrian girl in 1993 and lived in Vienna before being divorced again. Despite these wanderings he says that he is glad to be back in Morocco and living in Fez; he is now a tour guide. His English is pretty good and he adds one or two more Arabic words to my slowly growing vocabulary. We have been joined by Idriss, who says that he is also a tour guide and lives in Fez. He has been to university and is a Bachelor of Arts. He is a very impressive sight in his long black djellaba and neatly clipped beard. This little interlude is an important part of my travels for me, as it is always interesting to talk and share with people who are from different countries and ways of life.

There is a great banging of drums, and at the bottom of the dusty road I can see a man outside his shop with goods all around him on the floor outside. He is beating a large drum with much energy, obviously with the intention of getting customers interested. As I approach him he stares at me and says, 'You bought dagger from me.' I find this remarkable: I did indeed buy a dagger from him, but it must be nearly two years ago now.

I have found all Moroccans to be friendly and approachable, but when they find that you have visited their country before it seems as though they cannot do enough for you. His name is Abdul, and he is no exception. He ushers me into his shop and promises me better prices as someone who has bought from him before. There is a very nice necklace that I have my eye on for a present, and we start the process of haggling, which I love. Always have in your mind the maximum that you would pay and offer at least half of that at first; his first selling price would probably be in the region of four or five times that amount. The process of arriving at an agreed price is then not only an enjoyable experience but is also understood and respected by the seller. I get the necklace for about sixty per cent less than his starting price and we are both satisfied. We part with mutual salaams and he offers me the hospitality of his home if I pass this way again.

On the way to Moulay Idriss the single track road from Volubilis is winding up and up a very long and steep hill in a series of zigzags; it is a very picturesque route. We have been going downhill for some time now and shortly before we reach Moulay Idriss we stop for lunch at a wayside restaurant. Despite the heat I stick to my rule about eating the local dish when I travel to other countries; in this case it is beef tajine with carrot fritters and it is delicious.

Moulay Idriss

From outside the restaurant there is a lovely view of Moulay Idriss across the intervening valley. It is built on two hills that are part of Jebel Zerhoun (950 metres) and the buildings are gleaming white and cream in the bright sunlight. Moulay Idriss is Morocco's holiest city and was founded by Moulay Idriss I who established Morocco's first ruling dynasty; he lies buried in a mausoleum in the centre of the city. Every year in August there is a *Moussem* (religious festival) and thousands of pilgrims descend on the city to honour his memory.

The schedule is becoming a little tight because there is a train to catch from Meknes to Rabat later this afternoon; this means that sadly there will be no opportunity to stop in Moulay Idriss. The coach picks its way through the narrow and busy streets of this very interesting and attractive town, followed by a long climb out of the town with olive-covered mountains on one side and a vast fertile green plain on the other, also masses of prickly pear cactus once again. It is not a long journey to Meknes from here and shortly after joining the Meknes to Sidi Kacem road we cross the Meknes to Rabat railway line and enter the outskirts of Meknes itself.

There are men and women weeding huge areas of cultivated land by hand, and we pass a man herding a flock of intermingled goats and ducks. There is now a steady stream of traffic on what I thought was a dual carriageway but which turns out to be a long line of vehicles overtaking us and forcing the opposite traffic into the verge as a result. We are running along one side of a valley and on the other side is Meknes old town, surrounded by a wall some thirty feet high, similar to the one at Fez. A newly constructed dual carriageway, built on an embankment, also circles the town. This high part of Meknes is obviously the posh area with high walled gardens that screen lush green lawns, palm trees, bougainvillea and other brightly coloured shrubs.

Meknes old town

As we cross the valley and follow the road around the old town I am struck by the roundabouts that all have beautifully cut grass with palm trees and pink and red flowers, and are edged with red and white stones. We pass a garage with a 'Put a Tiger in your Tank' sign; it is a long time since I saw that logo! Just inside the city wall there is a lovely reservoir (Agdal Souani) and the blue water, the blue sky and the backdrop of the city walls make a lovely photograph.

We still have a little time. From here we are going to drive alongside the city walls and past Dar el-Makhzen (the royal palace) and then the golf course built by the late King Hassan II. We will also be able to see the mausoleum of Moulay Ismail (1672–1727) who made Meknes his capital and ordered the construction of the huge royal palace and a

Agdal Souani reservoir, Meknes

ring of ramparts with massive gates. The gates into the old town are very attractive with their clean beige colour and coloured mosaics. The one that I stop to photograph is actually two gates back to back, forming a battlemented entrance some thirty feet thick; some of the pillars used in the construction of these gates came from Volubilis.

Ben Khamis gate, Meknes

The city wall between these gates is at least thirty feet high and is in extremely good condition. By the famous sixteenth-century Bab Mansour gate there is a big open square where you can hire a horsedrawn carriage to explore this lovely old city at an appropriately sedate pace. A river (Oued Boukfrane) flows through Meknes with the old town on the west bank and the modern Meknes on the east bank.

Unfortunately we have no more time to explore this very interesting city and are soon on our way to the railway station. After passing a little shop called Chez Ali Baba we turn down a lovely avenue with beautiful mimosa trees on either side; the tranquillity is suddenly shattered by an open-back truck that squeezes past us with its horn blaring. Standing in the back are six or seven women in national dress, staring steadfastly forward with their highly colourful garments billowing behind them in the wind.

At Meknes station there is time for me to find a shop selling fruit, as so far I have missed my daily intake of bananas, apples and oranges. I manage to buy a supply of these at such a ridiculously cheap price that I add an enormous bunch of grapes as well. Back at the station I even have time for a cheese roll accompanied by a black coffee and a cup of mint tea. As is my custom I always try to interact with the local people and we exchange some words in Arabic and English.

Meknes station

Our train arrives

Another clean, fast and efficient rail transfer and we arrive in Rabat 6.45 pm. My hotel in Rabat is very nice indeed with lots of cool marble. I have a very luxurious room on the third floor with a beautiful view from my window across the river to Sale. By the time I have showered and changed and sampled the delightful Moroccan food on offer in the dining room I am ready for bed and am fast asleep by 10.00 pm.

* * *

I am up at 6.00 am. Although there is some cloud it promises to be another bright and hot day. I find my way to the roof where there is a small swimming pool and jacuzzi, and where it is possible to walk around the building and enjoy the fabulous views of the city, including the Hassan Tower which is only about half a mile away.

It is another busy day ahead with a morning sightseeing in Rabat followed by an afternoon train to Marrakech. The train journey to Marrakech will take most of the afternoon, and perhaps this is the moment to record that the train system in Morocco is all electrified (except the line from Sidi Kacem to Tangier), extremely fast and very efficient. All the locomotives that I have seen have been pulling at least twelve coaches and they have all been full; they are even building new lines.

Rabat is the capital of Morocco and the seat of its government. It lies on the south-west bank of the river Bou Regreg opposite the city of Sale on the north-east bank. Although Rabat is now a bustling and modern city, it is also a very old one and has many things of historic interest. My hectic morning includes visits to the mausoleum of Mohammed V, the Hassan Tower and the gardens and ruins of Chellah.

I am sitting outside the hotel at 8.30 in the morning, doing some people-watching while I await the arrival of the guide, and discover that this part of Rabat is much favoured by police and service personnel. Opposite is a café absolutely full of sailors. A man looking very like an admiral walks past but I think he is really some sort of senior policeman. A minibus across the road is full of policemen who are just sitting talking. On another side there are what I assume to be soldiers; they look very smart in beautifully pressed beige uniforms topped off with a beautiful white helmet; they also have white spats and white sleeve covers. Another group are also in beige uniforms but with green epaulets and green berets. Including the sailors in the café there must be at least fifty police and army personnel hanging around this crossroads.

Suddenly a young girl of about twenty-two walks past, dressed in a tight-fitting and low-cut black top and a very short black skirt; she has nice legs. All the people in the square are watching her, their eyes following her down the street and she knows it! She is walking down the middle of the road and is oblivious to the traffic. She turns a corner and is lost to sight and you can almost feel the onlookers relax.

Moroccan people are very friendly and one of the policemen comes over to talk with me. I greet him with '*Salaam alaykum*' and he becomes even friendlier and tells me about Rabat where he was born and has lived all his life. I tell him that I am on my way to Marrakech and he says that he has been there but prefers Rabat – because it is more modern, he says when I ask him.

We get under way and the first stop is the Merinid necropolis of Chellah, which lies in a valley and is completely surrounded by an extremely high and ancient wall. The Chellah was completed in the fourteenth century and stood on the site of the Roman settlement of Sala Colonia. Today it is a mixture of ruins, overgrown tombs, excavations, wild birds, exotic trees and flowers. The entrance is through an enormous gate with towers on each side that dwarf the wall; there are battlements on top of the towers and all along the wall. Inside, the path slopes down through beautiful trees including mimosa, palm, hibiscus and many other varieties. The sound of birds singing is everywhere.

There is a viewing platform with panoramic views of the river Bou Regreg with Sale on the other side. Here, I am accosted by a ginger, white and black cat that is demanding my attention; he approaches me with his tail erect and a purposeful stare. Down on my haunches, I get a nice face-on photograph of him, and later a canine compatriot of his.

My new friend

Not dead, just dead tired

Further down are the ruins of Chellah and the mosque, and on top of the ruined minaret there is a large nest with a stork standing upright in it. It is very evocative as I walk among these ruins and forgotten tombs, some of which are covered in creepers. As I make my way along a narrow path, brushing beautiful hibiscus flowers out of my way, there is a tremendous sense of peace. It seems a shame to have to leave this place and enter the bustle of life outside those huge gates.

We follow the Boulevard Hassan round and arrive outside the great courtyard that contains the Hassan Tower and the mausoleum of Mohammed V. The entrance is guarded by two men on white horses;

The ruins of Chellah

River Bou Regreg from Chellah (and stork's nest}

they are also dressed entirely in white except for a green hat inlaid with white diamond patterns. Each of them is holding a lance with a small green flag at the end. They make an impressive sight and are happy to have their photograph taken, although remuneration is expected.

Guards at the mausoleum of Mohammed V

The tower is 144 feet high with walls eight feet thick, and construction of it was started by Yakub al-Mansur in 1195 with the intention that it would be the minaret of a huge mosque big enough to contain the entire army for prayers. When Yakub died four years later work was abandoned and today the unfinished tower stands at the sea end of a huge paved courtyard containing 200 columns between six and ten feet high that indicate the outline of the planned mosque.

The Hassan Tower

At the other end of the courtyard is the mausoleum of Mohammed V. It is a beautiful white building with intricately worked stone horseshoe arches and a pointed green roof. There is a broad sweep of marble stairs leading to the entrance which is guarded by a single man dressed in a white tunic with brass buttons and baggy white trousers; a flowing white cloak and green and red hat complete the outfit. He is armed with what looks to me to be an extremely ancient musket. Inside, it is very cool and tranquil, and the white and beige marble casket sits in the middle of an intricately laid floor some 20 feet below the mezzanine floor from which we look down.

The mausoleum of Mohammed V

Below and beyond the courtyard of the Hassan Tower, and between there and the river, there are a lot of environmental changes with great swathes of newly laid grass and many palm trees being planted. Everywhere there is colour, with flowers of purple, yellow, blue, pink, white and red, and also a lot of little white egrets just standing around. The intention is to create an area of great pleasure and enjoyment with open parkland around the river, a marina and shops and parks with beautiful trees and flowers, linked by walkways and boulevards. This area will also be served by a new electric metro link between Sale and Rabat.

The last visit, before I head for Rabat railway station and the train to Marrakech, is to Rabat medina, which dates from the seventeenth century; it stands on top of a hill overlooking Rabat with the Atlantic to the north and the river to the east.

Rabat from the old medina

Inside the old medina at Rabat

There are no shops or traders, just a maze of very narrow residential streets with the houses painted in white and blue. However, there is a small café at the end, and sitting drinking coffee, eating freshly made biscuits and looking at the river with Sale on the other side is a very relaxing pastime.

View of Sale from Rabat old medina

On the way out of the medina there is a little shop selling freshly made orange juice. The owner is a very laid-back sort of person and says that it is his philosophy in life. It seems to be shared by the two workmen sitting relaxed in the shade next to him. They are all nice people and are very happy for me to take their photograph.

Fresh orange juice on sale

There are now just fifty minutes before the train departs, and the only sights left to see in Rabat will be during the drive to the station. There is no time to stop, and views sometimes slip by too quickly to record although we are slowed down as we enter the Andalusian quarter. There are a lot of artistic things going on here, such as a shop making and selling silver jewellery. A man at the roadside is making the little inlaid octagonal tables that fold up after you remove the top; I used to have one but alas it is no more. Another shop is selling things carved from wood, including birds, figures and even small furniture. Down another street and all the shops in this one are selling pictures and objets d'art, then another street that is all clothes shops.

There is as much on show outside as inside, and there is a profusion of colours and styles dancing from lines strung across the front of the shops.

The last time that I was in Rabat railway station it was a modern and immaculate building with a gleaming terrazzo floor in its upper hall; there was also a nice restaurant and good information facilities. Today it is a building site with lots of dust and a temporary walkway but from the huge display board of what it will look like when finished it seems that Rabat will indeed have a station fitting for the capital of the country. Escalators take you down to the platforms and the lines run through what is a deep cutting between buildings; there are palm trees and greenery everywhere and everything is spotless. The trains enter and leave the station through tunnels under the city and at the entrance to each tunnel there are castellated sandstone walls.

Rabat station

The train is another gleaming Hitachi locomotive in yellow and red, and is again pulling a long line of coaches in matching livery. From Rabat to Casablanca the distance is approximately 100 kilometres and the line runs parallel to the Atlantic all that way. From Casablanca to Benguerir, a distance of approximately 170 kilometres, the view from

Zahir offers me lunch on the train

the carriage window, on both sides, is an unending one of wheat and barley crops. At Benguerir there is another railway line that goes to Safi on the coast.

I get into conversation with a man at the end of the corridor who is smoking a cigarette, despite the no smoking sign. His name is Damino and he owns a company that makes high-quality glass products; when I say, like Murano, he says yes. He is Italian and in addition to his own language he speaks fluent French, English, German and some Arabic and has houses in Lido de Jesolo, Venice and Marrakech. He expresses great interest in the fact that I travel round the world on railway trains, and he tells me about some of the magnificent railway journeys to be had in Switzerland and Austria, as well as Italy. He asks me a lot about Peru and I jokingly ask why he doesn't consider branching out his business to there. This brings a thoughtful expression to his face; not such a joke after all.

Outside the view is now of much wheat. There is an economical and efficient way of protecting the crop from animals, as the fields are surrounded by prickly pear cactus plants, guaranteed to keep most things out I should think. Our passing startles a flock of white egrets. Here we are about thirty minutes from Marrakech; the Atlas Mountains are now clearly visible in the distance and look hard and unyielding. The view changes again, with mines on one side and on the other a construction site for a new railway line, I am not sure where to. Marrakech is now pretty close and the immediate landscape is quite different, looking like a plain of red sandy grit rather than soil. It changes again and now resembles a bomb-site, waste ground pitted with large holes and lots of lumps of concrete lying about. There are many goats wandering around and I can't help wondering what on earth they find to eat in this barren place. The view changes to a construction site of square apartment blocks and this view goes on, quite literally for miles, until we are suddenly in Marrakech station; there must have been hundreds and hundreds of those buildings.

In and around Marrakech new station

This is not only the terminus of the railway but also the last time that I will travel by train on this particular journey through Morocco. There is now a gleaming brand new station here, with lots of marble. The hundreds of people who get off the train now pass through a booking hall more reminiscent of the inside of a grand mosque than a railway station. From the spotless marble floor to the high carved ceiling above it is impressive, and there is also a lot of glass and mosaic work.

It is four o'clock and after the coolness of the train the heat radiating from the paved forecourt is rather a shock. I am also tired and looking forward to a refreshing shower. The hotel is only a short drive away and is the four star El Andalous on the Avenue President Kennedy. This hotel is big, smart and very nice: the decoration is traditional and there is a lovely swimming pool. My room is a large double with an outside balcony, with table and chairs where I can sit and relax overlooking the luxurious greenery of the garden.

Hotel El Andalous entrance, pool and garden

The very name Marrakech conjures up the image of something mysterious and exotic, and inside the walls of the old town there are numerous narrow alleys that enhance that feeling and remind you that Marrakech has a thousand years of history behind it. Before Rabat became the official capital of Morocco in 1913, several cities had claimed that title including Marrakech. Although that ancient and long-running dispute over which city was the capital has now been settled, Marrakech today is still the most important city in the south of the country, and is the gateway to the Sahara.

Away to the east, the Atlas Mountains dominate the horizon and the highest summit in that range, Jebel Toubkal, is only some thirty miles away. Although Marrakech is Morocco's second oldest city, and there is a wealth of mediaeval history and buildings, the steady influx of western tourists is having its effect. Away from the centre of the city and the medina, great swathes of land are being covered in high-quality and expensive hotels, linked by beautifully paved roads lined with palm trees and flowers.

I will be staying here for another two nights, and this will be the chance for some relaxation after the hectic rush of the last few days. I plan to visit Place Djemaa el Fna (Square of the Dead) this afternoon; this is very much the nerve centre of Marrakech. Behind it stands the twelfth-century La Koutoubia Mosque (Mosque of the Booksellers); at 230 feet it towers over the medina. Djemaa el Fna was originally the place where criminals were executed and their severed heads hung up for all to see.

This morning there is a tour of the Bahia Palace and surrounds. At the palace gate we are greeted by our guide, Abdul. He is impressively tall and is wearing a long flowing purple djellaba. We met here once before many months ago and it is nice to renew a friendship. There is a wide paved walkway from the entrance with all sorts of different trees on each side and as it widens out to a courtyard at the end there is a huge trailing purple bougainvillea in full bloom. The trees here provide some welcome shade from the hot sun, although there are several expectant cats sitting in a circle in the full sun.

The entrance to Bahia Palace

Bahia Palace was built in 1894 by Abu Ahmed with craftsmen from Fez and was supposed to have been the greatest palace of its time. It did eventually become the residence of the colonial French governor but largely fell into disuse after that, although even today its lovely stucco work, mosaic paths and walks, and beautifully carved cedar ceilings are there to be seen and enjoyed. There are many doorways and reception halls, and passing through one we come on a huge courtyard with a central basin. On all sides there are rooms that were originally intended for the concubines. There is restoration work going on so the basin is empty of water, and a lot of the area has restricted access. The secluded courtyards with palms, bougainvillea and orange trees, criss-crossed with mosaic paths, make this palace and its faded grandeur an oasis of peace, beauty and tranquillity in this busy city.

The old harem

Basking cats

Abdul now leads us to the sixteenth-century Bahia Palace, built by Saadian Sultan Ahmed el Monsour. When it was completed, it was described as one of the world's most beautiful buildings. However, the vast majority of it was destroyed when the Saadian dynasty fell in 1659 and Marrakech was ransacked. The Saadain tombs were rediscovered in 1917, and are now open to visitors and a popular part of the tourist trail.

Bahia Palace

Storks on the palace walls

Passing through the entrance I find that it is just a large open area with several sunken orange groves and little else. On all sides there is a very high crumbling red stone wall. Along the top of one of the perimeter walls I can count sixteen huge nests each with a resident stork, and as in Volubilis there is the sound of clacking beaks. There is a system of underground tunnels and dungeons but it is not possible to see those today. In one corner there are some rather steep stairs and these lead up to a terrace from which there is a lovely view of Marrakech; it is also possible to get a closer view of some of the storks.

Despite the lack of buildings or other features inside it is still a very impressive place. When I tell Abdul this he asks me for an explanation of 'impressive'. He listens attentively and his pronunciation of the word is extremely good; he says that he will use it in future tours.

I wander off to look for Said, who has a small shop close to Djemaa el Fna selling beautiful bags, cushions, tassels and clothing. His shop is small but a riot of colour. As I have met him before, he is very welcoming and insists on me sitting on a minute chair while he disappears, only to reappear after a few minutes with the traditional tray of mint tea. In this little corner of the busy medina it is very nice to relax with yet another new friend in Morocco and time passes quickly although that is of no consequence. I buy a delightful Berber shoulder bag and get his business card with his photo on it, and we part with mutual salaams and a promise to visit him again when I return to Morocco.

With thoughts of new recipes to cook at home my next port of call is another small shop on the edge of the square, to meet Khasam and buy spices. He is the same friendly man that I met last time. The spices are all beautifully arranged in conical piles in drums outside his shop and the colours and smells are almost intoxicating. I end up with 200 grams each of fresh cumin, saffron, lemon curry, tajine and coriander for the ridiculous price of about £4.50. More salaams and I am on my way again.

There is a huge variety of things for sale in the narrow labyrinth of streets in the medina with spices, cloth, silver and leather apparently being the most popular. Very little happens in Djemaa el Fna before noon but from then on it becomes more and more frenetic until by evening time there are stall holders and entertainers everywhere with hundreds of onlookers or participants.

On the square itself I end up on one of the stalls that are selling fresh orange juice, and here I meet Khalid. He is delightfully loud and

Spices for sale

friendly; he shouts, 'Oh la la,' and thinks it is wonderful to have me beside him while he harangues the passers-by to buy his orange juice. We part with a typical Moroccan embrace and a promise from me to buy more of his orange juice later in the day.

Khalid and his oranges

Just off the square there is the nice rooftop restaurant Islane, the perfect place for lunch. Sitting here with my lamb tajine with dried figs and walnuts I can see the snow-capped Atlas Mountains through the heat haze; they are 40 miles from here and the view of them shimmers and changes in the heat rather like a mirage. It seems a bit odd to be sitting here in a temperature nearing 90°F, looking at snow.

Later I am sitting on a low wall under the trees enjoying the shade where the horse carriages are parked. As I sit idly looking at nothing I notice that the driver of one of the carriages has a brush and pot of black paint; he is touching up the horses legs with it and I wonder whether the black horse is really black.

The horse-drawn carriages are known as caleches, and remind me of that song about the Surrey with a Fringe on Top. I decide to hire one

Caleches

for an hour to drive round the old medina and the royal palace. The driver is young man of about eighteen who laughs when I ask if the horses are his own; he says that he has a patron. On average he does about four trips a day for about £18 each. He doesn't tell me what his percentage of that is. I am able to sit on top with him and the drive is delightful, a lovely way to see this part of Marrakech.

I decide that, as it is still fairly early, I will have a quick wash and change of shirt and then head back to another part of the old medina that I did not see earlier, then go on to the Djemaa el Fna for the evening festivities. The taxi drops me off by the square and although it is only about two or three hours since I left, it is already considerably busier and very crowded. Several mobile stalls have arrived, all providing a sit-down eating service and very busy with customers. The sights are many and varied; a first for me is watching a snake charmer enticing a nasty-looking cobra out of a basket by playing music to it on a little flute.

Street entertainment

There are many stalls that are just selling oranges and the fruit is stacked in perfectly symmetrical pyramids. There are jugglers, one of whom is whirling at least five or six balls into the air at one time, marvellous how he keeps them all going. As an obvious westerner I am a target for souvenir sellers and there is a persistent young man in a long white djellaba type garment who is convinced that my life will not be complete unless I buy a fez from him, I try it on and he smiles. In the gathering dusk a lady swathed in clothes, and sitting under a very large umbrella, offers to tell my fortune. I smile and walk away but later wished that I had tried it.

Afternoon in and around Djemaa el Fna

The square is now getting quite dark but all the stalls are brilliantly lit and those selling dried fruit and nuts are bright splashes of colour. I am next attracted by a large crowd gathered in the centre of the square. When I squeeze through the crowd (I am the only westerner in it) I can see two men squaring up to each other, each with a vicious-looking cudgel. I cannot believe that this is only entertainment as they proceed to belabour each other, apparently without mercy.

Cudgels on Djemaa el Fna at night

A spice stall

La Koutoubia mosque at night

A young boy of about fifteen is giving a display of fire eating; a torrent of yellow and red flame is coming from the liquid that ignites as it leaves his mouth. What a way to earn a living. There are acrobats, storytellers and magicians and also several men wandering about dressed in costumes rather like pantomime pirates, I am not sure what they are about. It is now quite dark. There are many food stalls, each one with a group of customers seated in a row on each side; there are no empty spaces at any of them. The snake charmers must still be in business as I can hear the noise of their pipes even over the tremendous hubbub of the square. There is also a steady thud thud of drums and the occasional blast from something like a hunting horn.

Standing in the midst of this throbbing mass of humanity and noise is both exhilarating and exhausting. As I have been here some five hours I think it is time to beat a retreat for the sanctuary of my hotel. Nevertheless, I am glad that I did not miss the experience of Djemaa el Fna at night.

A very nice dinner in the hotel restaurant, with no beef burgers or chips in sight, and then yet another early night, although I spend time catching up with my notes as the adrenalin rush from the sights and sounds of Djemaa el Fna is keeping sleep at bay.

* * *

Up at 6.30 am to another beautiful day with a bright blue sky and some fluffy white clouds. It is going to be hot again but at least today there is a refreshing breeze. Today I am going to explore the old medina.

The taxi drops me off at yet another of the massive gates that are a feature of all the old towns and cities in Morocco. Inside it is a panorama of sights and sounds with virtually everyone in traditional dress, and as I plunge into the narrow alleys and small squares the smell of meat and fish is almost overpowering. In addition, there are stalls selling spices, clothes, carpets, fruit and vegetables, silver, kitchen utensils and many other things. Most of the meat stalls have a queue of women waiting to be served. It appears that no part of the carcass is wasted; one of the meat stalls even has a complete sheep's head and its eyes seem to glare at me balefully as I walk past.

Pedestrians and riders on bicycles and mopeds jostle for space in the narrow shopping alleys but there is no sense of frustration or anger.

Inside the old medina

Outside one of the alleys there are a group of old women sitting on the floor with their backs against the wall. They are not begging but are staring very intently at something, although I cannot see what it is. They are all wearing traditional dress but are not veiled; at the end of the line of women there is a single man sitting with his arms crossed and looking a bit self-conscious.

In the main street through the medina, although there are a few cars, the main mode of transport is mopeds and they buzz up and down like flies. High on the top of a ruined building two storks stand proudly in their nest and impassively survey the crowds below.

Spot the storks

I am followed for some time by a lady in full national costume, including veil, and to escape her attentions I enter a little shop that is selling fossils, marble cats and masks, some of which are quite intimidating. I make the acquaintance of an elderly gentleman called Abd er Rahman, and his assistant Rahaal; there is no pressure to buy anything and they invite me to take mint tea with them. I greet them in Arabic but when they respond enthusiastically I explain that I have now shot my linguistic

Abd er Rahman and Rahaal and their shop

bolt in that language. They then proceed to teach me a few more words and I return the favour, although their English is considerably better than my Arabic. It is a very pleasant cultural exchange, with each of us interested to know more about the other. Although I bought some items I felt, and so did they I think, that the transaction was secondary to the exchange of friendship.

Lady of mystery

Outside, my veiled friend is still waiting and she again waves necklaces and bracelets before me. I have to say that they are very nice and I buy several of them at what is a very reasonable price. In exchange she allows me to take a photograph of her.

Transport ancient and modern

As I wait outside the Medina gates for a taxi back to the hotel there is a wonderful mixture of transport going past, which includes smart horse-drawn landaus, shiny Mercedes cars, noisy little mopeds, a donkey and cart, and the odd bus.

I am sorry to leave this wonderful part of Marrakech, as I have felt part of it, but tomorrow is the start of a 400-mile journey south and I have things to do before then, such as writing notes, telephoning home and packing, not to mention another superb dinner.

I seem to be making a habit of waking up at 6.00 am but it is an eight o'clock start for the first leg to Ouarzazate. As we leave Marrakech behind, the country becomes quite flat and featureless and the houses are mostly box-shaped and painted pink; Marrakech is known as the 'pink city'.

About 25 miles from Marrakech we pass through Ait Ourir. We are already in the foothills of the High Atlas, and this small town appears little changed by time, with transport for people and goods being almost exclusively mules. There is a man herding goats alongside the road but they are all indifferent to our passing. A woman clad in black from head to toe is riding a donkey side-saddle. The only modern thing here is the tarmac road through the town.

Through the High Atlas

As we head higher into the Atlas we pass several roadside stalls selling fossils: they are big on fossils in Morocco. One sign reads 'Stop fossil'. We are high above a tree-covered valley where villages cling to the mountainside; a man is loading two large barrels of water strapped onto the sides of a mule. In some cases great distances are travelled to bring water in this way, although some villages do have a well from which water is drawn from about 25 feet below the surface.

All the people that live in this area are Berbers and the basic income in these small villages is from agriculture and their goats and sheep. If they need anything extra then they take a goat or sheep to market. In the drier parts of the High Atlas, children are sent out to search for water. The traditional way that the houses are built is of layers of clay, pebbles and straw, although some are made from mud bricks.

When it comes to transport no space is wasted: we pass a man herding a mule laden with straw, so much of it that it appears to be just an enormous pile of straw with four tiny legs sticking out at the bottom. A little later we are behind an open-backed truck that is so packed with sheep you could not get a hand between them. In the middle of this tightly packed flock is a man and as the truck sways from side to side on the bends the whole load moves as one, like some orchestrated movement.

We reach Tizi-n-Tichka and there is a short stop to stretch legs and take photographs of the road far below us, as this is the highest vehicular pass in Morocco at 2260 metres. The road over Tizi-n-Tichka was built by the French in 1936.

Tizi-n-Tichka

Some twenty miles to the east of here is the kasbah Telouet. This was once the seat of the Glaoui warlords who not only controlled the caravan route from Marrakech to Ouarzazate but also most of the High Atlas. The most well-known of these chieftains was Thami el-Glaoui whom the French made pasha of Marrakech, only for him to be deposed and his property confiscated in 1956 following independence.

We continue to drop down from Tizi-n-Tichka and are following the course of a river in a valley. The ground is a rich chocolate colour, some terraced to preserve moisture but I cannot tell whether it is medieval or recent. Across the valley there is a village in the cleft of a hill; a red village clinging to a red hillside – perfect camouflage.

A little further on we pass through a bustling little wayside town called Agouim, where there are several shops selling fruit, vegetables, meat, and clay pots, and women are working in the fields among the walnut trees. The houses are very low, very flat and very red; the roofs are only made of mud and straw, and on some of the houses the roof

The red village

appears to be growing. Along the roadside are more stalls selling fossils and clay pots, and nearby there are rugs lying flat on the hillside to dry.

Sales time

The road from here to Amerzgane is very poor but it does not seem to be affecting the driver as he continues to press on at 80 kph. There are more settlements about now and there is a fertile-looking valley on my left; this seems to be where the waters of the river rise to the surface once more. Where there is off-road space and shade there is often a little stall set up selling trays of fossils or sometimes tired-looking fruit. There are people washing in the river bed, and also beating clothes on the stones; masses of brightly coloured clothes laid out on the rocks to dry.

A ruined settlement appears on the side of the road. The buildings have been weathered into fantastic shapes, rather like some form of abstract art. On the mountain behind the settlement there has been a landslide and it is like a great terracotta-coloured wound in its side. We are now only 35 kilometres from Ouarzazate and have reached Amerzgane;

at this point the main road turns off to Agadir but we continue onwards for a few kilometres and then take a side road to Ait Benhaddou. Many people will have seen Ait Benhaddou without knowing where it is or what it is called, for it has featured in movies such as *Lawrence of Arabia*, *Gladiator* and *Romancing the Stone.*

The town from above Ait Benhaddou

The town stands on a hill on one side of a very wide river bed and the kasbah of Ait Benhaddou is built into the side of a hill on the opposite side. There is a timeless beauty about the town, which was once a bustling and wealthy place but now the narrow packed-earth streets are eerily quiet. As the path wends its way down to the river the only signs of life are some places selling jewellery and other souvenirs. I am invited into one of the shops but am not pressured to buy anything by the traditionally dressed Berber. We exchange greetings and I admire some of the quite exquisite necklaces, brooches and other items that line the wall of his small and traditionally built house. There follows some good-natured haggling but even his starting price I think is very reasonable and I buy several items including a silver necklace set with a beautiful black stone.

Ait Benhaddou

By the river bed there are a group of young boys standing at the edge of what is just a trickle of water some six feet wide and a few inches deep. They are obviously there to try and make a dirham or two, and the way they go about it you would think that they are assisting you in crossing a raging torrent.

The ferry to the kasbah

On the other side stands the magnificent kasbah of Ait Benhaddou, truly one of the finest in Morocco. The elaborately decorated towers of red stone and the mud brick walls stand timeless in the sun, and with its skirt of palm trees and a cloudless blue sky behind, it is little wonder that people want to film here. As I wander round inside it is like going back in time: the houses are built of mud and stone and the narrow streets are a mixture of shale and clay, doorways are just holes cut into the wall and there is no evidence of any modern amenity, except for one small place selling postcards. When it was built they obviously used the hillside, as many of the streets inside the kasbah are very steep and it is decidedly hot work exploring. I find a small deserted house; it has no windows and just a hole in the wall for a doorway and when I creep

Inside Ait Benhaddou

into its very dark interior I am surprised at just how cool it is, remembering that it is at least 100 degrees Fahrenheit outside. The complex covers several acres and although people live in the kasbah I only saw three, all men, and all traditionally dressed Berbers.

We reach the outskirts of Ouarzazate and pass the Atlas Film Studios, a product of all the film-making attention that this area gets. As we enter the town we drive down a road lined on both sides with tamarisk trees and on reaching the hotel, which is on top of a hill, there is a good view of the town below. Despite the fact that it was only built in 1928 there is a traditional look to the town.

Ouarzazate

Hotel Kenzi Azghor

My hotel is the Kenzi Azghor and at the front there are two enormous date palms that are laden with fruit. Close to the beautiful terracotta courtyard with its central fountain there is a pomegranate tree literally bowed down with fruit: I didn't take one, but was tempted.

Ouarzazate is some 130 miles south of Marrakech. It was a garrison town built by the French in 1928 and today it is a provincial capital and stands alongside a large artificial lake that was created by damming the river Draa. It is at the head of two valleys and is an oasis in the middle of very barren country. From here the two main routes to the Sahara are through the Vallee Du Draa to Zagora and Tagounite, or the one that I am taking which is along the Vallee Du Dades to Tinejdad and Erfoud. Along that route will be a stop to see the magnificent Todra Gorge.

I am up at 6.00 am again to another beautiful day although it promises to be very hot later on. Good dinner last night of beef, potatoes and cheese. We leave Ouarzazate and pass through a very barren landscape with rock formations close to the road; the rest is just a red, brown and grey gravelly area on all sides. We pass a group of four or five children all about eight years old, just sitting at the roadside. They don't appear to be selling anything. As far as the eye can see in any direction there is no sign of people or human habitation, or even greenery. I cannot but help wonder what brought them to that desolate and inhospitable spot.

The view goes on unchangingly until suddenly on a hill there is a kasbah surrounded by date palms and trees, and we make a short stop close by to buy some water at a wayside shop. It is too hot to trudge up the hill to the kasbah and I sip my cold water under the shade of an old and extremely gnarled tamarisk tree.

The kasbah and the tamarisk

We pass through Skoura, an oasis town, without stopping. The road from here just seems to go on and on though this barren pebbly wilderness without end, until suddenly we are entering El-Kelaa M'Gouna in Vallée des Roses (the valley of the roses). El-Kelaa M'Gouna was a garrison town for the French; its current population is approximately 10,000 and although there are some side streets most of it sprawls on each side of the road for a considerable distance. There are lots of cars and cafés and plenty of people about. This is an area with plenty of water, and in the spring the fields are an enormous mass of rose pink petals from which is made perfume, rose water and soap, enough to provide for the whole country. Presumably it also provides much needed employment in this area.

El-Kelaa M'Gouna

At a little shop on a side street I exchange greetings with the shopkeeper, and while I am buying some rose-scented soap to take home, the man behind the counter tells me that there is a rose festival in May each year to celebrate the harvest of petals and the benefit that they bring to the town. As we are talking a woman with bowed head, clothed entirely in white, walks past. In response to my query he says that when Moroccan women mourn for a dead husband they dress entirely in white and mourn for 4 months and 10 days.

We move on through Boumaine-du-Dades and reach Tinehir where there is a stop for lunch. This is at the Kasbah Hotel Lamrani which, although obviously new, is constructed like a kasbah with high walls and a large red double doorway into the courtyard. On each side there is a tower and the building is an attractive dusky pink colour with white decorative stone work on the top of the walls and towers.

Tinehir is an extremely green and fertile oasis with many palm trees and areas of cultivation, and is one of the largest oases in Morocco. It nestles between the green abundance of the oasis and the arid and barren slopes of the Moyen Atlas. It is also famous for the quality of the silver Berber jewellery that you can buy here and the old castle of the Glaoui clan on top of a nearby hill. Tinehir is a growing place, as in addition to income from agriculture and tourism, Moroccan people who have worked in Europe have brought money back. Prices are going higher and higher, and in some parts you can pay up to 6000 dirham (about £375) per square metre for land.

In the hotel grounds there is an area set aside where there is a very large Bedouin tent, and lunch is taken in it. The floor, walls and ceiling are covered with intricately patterned rich carpets; the food and the atmosphere are all traditional and the whole thing is a very pleasant experience. On the return trip we will spend the night here, but now it is time to head for the Todra Gorge.

Todra Gorge is one of the sights of Morocco that all tourists should see and experience. Having read about it beforehand I am full of anticipation as we pick our way carefully along the single-track road from Tinehir. The gorge is about ten miles from Tinehir and all along this road are thousands of date palms and cultivated land sustained by the river that flows to the gorge. The crops are quite numerous and include cereal, barley, carrots, vegetables and grass for the animals. There are also walnut and fig trees in abundance.

On the road to Todra Gorge

There are several kasbahs and I spot two impromptu stalls at the side of the road where brightly coloured rugs, mats and scarves can be bought. There are numerous guesthouses and hotels to accommodate the many people that come to see this place.

Suddenly you are in the gorge and two sheer cliffs rise to a thousand feet on each side of you. The blue grey river is flowing alongside the road, which in some places has been concreted to accommodate the increase in tourist traffic. In one place it crosses the road and little concrete markers show where the edge is.

At one point the canyon is only thirty feet wide. As I walk along, it is quite cool after the heat of the desert; the water too is cold, ice cold,

Tondra Gorge

and is fed by the snows of the High Atlas. In some places you can see where the water is seeping from the mountain and creating additional pools to the river. There is water everywhere. High above me the peaks of the gorge are bathed in hot Moroccan sunshine but here, hundreds of feet below, the sunshine only penetrates for a brief period each morning. This is a spectacular place.

Across the river on a narrow piece of shingle beach there are two men wrapped in blankets, fast asleep. A lorry passes, laden to the gunwales with pieces of burnt eucalyptus tree destined to be made into charcoal. At the side of the road there are two tethered mules nibbling at a small pile of bark that has been stripped from trees, and sitting on the ground is a woman dressed in black, openly breastfeeding a baby. Around her are some carrier bags and bottles of water, and you get the distinct impression that this is the sum total of her possessions. She asks for money and perhaps I am overgenerous, but then I would not want to swap places with her.

At the end of the gorge, and reached by a bridge of two planks on some stones, is the Hotel Yasmina. It is very modern but built in the

Life in the gorge

kasbah style. Another piece of modernity is on the walls of the gorge where, in some places, somebody has spray-painted their name. I find it difficult to understand how someone could be interested enough to come and see this wonderful place, and then deface it when they get here.

From here to Tinejdad is about 40 miles and the view is always the same: barren stony ground and the mountains in the background. There are a lot of palm trees in Tinejdad; there are also a lot of bicycle repair shops and children riding bicycles. It is a busy little town almost entirely confined to both sides of the road that runs through it. Craftsmen are working outside their shops and I can see a man making wardrobes and beds and another welding some form of implement. They are not all working, as I can also see a group of men around a roadside café table gesticulating and arguing about something – maybe who pays the bill, but I doubt it.

All the lorries and pick-ups that pass us are very ancient and the occasional JCB-type diggers are derelict-looking and rusty. It doesn't look as though there is much employment in this town. We turn off the main road at Tinejdad and are now on the last leg to Erfoud, but make a brief stop to photograph the wells of an underground irrigation system that goes back hundreds of years and was based on a Persian design. The land around us is flat and barren as far as the eye can see, except for the openings to these wells which are just very deep holes with the earth thrown up around them, rather like huge mole hills. There are literally hundreds of them. I stand near the edge of one of them to take a photograph. The ground is dry and crumbly and, on impulse, I throw a small stone into the void and wait in vain for the sound of it landing. I move back hurriedly as I cannot imagine anyone falling into one of these wells ever being rescued.

Back at the minibus there are two Berbers waiting to sell fossils. A

The wells

few minutes ago there was not a soul in sight and there is no sign of any other transport. It is as if they just shot up out of the ground.

We reach Touroug, which is a poor-looking dusty little town with lots of children about. A group of them, all about twelve years old, play football and the game appears to be being refereed by a man on a horse. We drive quite slowly and pass a man in a dirty yellow jersey trotting along on a mule with another man cycling alongside him, both of them very easy-paced and chatting away. A boy of about ten cycles past, he is standing on the pedals and looks a bit tired. No wonder, he has a passenger in the shape of a grown man sitting very relaxed on the back, riding side-saddle. All the women around here are dressed totally in black. Just at the end of the town there is a large patch of damp-looking ground which appears to be mainly sand. A man is trudging behind a mule which is pulling what seems to be just a piece of wood rather that anything that might be called a plough. It is not clear what the crop might be. Touroug is a point where two rivers meet, and in this area there are acres and acres of date palms.

I suppose some people might see Touroug as being without interest, but to me it is a picture of everyday life in a remote little town in the deep south of Morocco. Apart from the railway aspect of my journey, it is the type of thing that I have come to see, along with the many historical and architectural places and points of interest.

It is now only about ten miles to Erfoud and a welcome dinner and bed. Although the journey from Marrakech has been extremely interesting and enjoyable, it has also been long and tiring and not helped by the heat, but before it ends there is one more town of note, and that is Jorf.

Jorf is quite a big place and there are lots of kasbahs, one or two of them ruined. There is a market in full swing with many people; all the women here are also dressed completely in black.

We reach Erfoud and the gateway to the Sahara: journey's end for today. The Kasbah Hotel Xaluca Maadid is four kilometres on the other side of the town and during the drive it seems as though every person in Erfoud owns a white Land Rover – there are dozens of them. This is because the main source of income is tourism and for that you must have a vehicle that will take you into the desert. Everything here is about tourism and the paved roads lined with tamarisk trees are very busy: there are petrol stations, cafés, places to change money, hotels, banks, restaurants, street telephones (lots of them), ice cream booths, shops and garages. The main transport for the locals appears to be bicycles.

Outside the hotel there is a long line of white Land Rovers and beside each one is a man in a white *djellaba*; with the hotel being built like a kasbah with towers and high walls with battlements surrounding an extensive courtyard, it looks rather like an elaborate film set. This feeling is heightened when you get inside, as there is a swimming pool with dazzling underwater lighting and a sunken bar; everywhere there are palm trees and exotic shrubs. Dinner tonight is a buffet outside, and the selection of traditional food is excellent as is the company. Friend and stranger alike, we all sit at a huge long table. During the meal a man appears leading a camel, which he proceeds to walk around the table with the apparent intention of introducing the beast to everyone individually. I find it a very novel and enjoyable experience but not everyone shares my feeling.

I have a restless night as the air conditioning is not very effective and the room is very hot. At about 2.30 am I decide to give in and get up, with the result that I am washed, dressed and at the breakfast table by 3.30 am. This is not as terrible as it sounds, as we are due for a call at 3.30 anyway for the one-hour drive in a four-by-four vehicle over rough desert to Merzouga, to meet up with a group of Berbers who will lead us into the Sahara to watch the sunrise over the mountains of Algeria.

We are off at 4.00 am, and as we leave the town area it soon becomes rough desert and the ride is both fast and bumpy. The driver drives with confidence and sees a track where no track seems to exist, as his powerful headlights cut a dazzling swathe through the darkness.

At about a quarter to five we reach the camp of the Berbers; this is as far as the Land Rover goes.

As I climb gratefully out of the Land Rover I can see vague forms and hear snuffling noises and grunts; this is my next method of transport. Berbers in traditional dress move silently about. One of them has a torch and the eyes of the camels shine green in its light. He introduces me to my mount and says that the camel's name is Osama and that he is a good camel. Osama looks at me dispassionately and continues to chew with his thick rubbery lips; I have never been on a camel before and hope that Osama will not take advantage of my inexperience.

The secret of staying on when the camel gets up is to go with his movement and not against it. I am suddenly high above the ground and ready to go. This is the point at which I have half expected to end up back on the ground and now, perched high on this camel's back, I am feeling quite pleased with myself. Osama, however, continues to look bored.

Here we go

We leave this area of flat, hard-packed sand and the camels plod off with a swinging gait in single file. Ahead of us is a forty-minute trek over the dunes into the Sahara proper, to reach a point at which I can sit on top of a dune and watch the sunrise. I have been waiting eagerly for this moment, but it does not take away the thrill of the experience of trekking in a genuine desert. It is a wonderful experience, padding along under the starlit skies, the only sound the occasional creaking of the leather harness. The silence affects you, and I stifle a question that I want to ask the Berber walking silently at my side.

To my surprise our little convoy suddenly comes to a halt. I can't believe that forty minutes of this very silent journey have now ended. In the lea of some dunes the camels are settled down with their legs tucked under them, and the last lap of this journey is for me to climb one of the large dunes in front of me. The Sahara sand is a rich reddish

Magical sunrise

The empty desert

colour and is very, very fine. It is very hard work climbing to the top of this dune.

At the top, the Berber is determined to make this an experience for me to enjoy and from somewhere produces a blanket for me to sit on. Although I would have been just as happy to sit on the sand, I feel it would be discourteous to refuse and I accept his offer in Arabic. This seems to spur him on to other gestures and he removes his blue robe and turban and proceeds to dress me in them. It might seem to be vanity but I consider that the finished look does not look too bad.

The sky is now starting to slowly lighten. Bit by bit that light strengthens until suddenly I can see the tip of the sun peeping over the mountains on the other side of the border. The silence is absolute. I watch spellbound as the sun grows and chases away the mists and darkness, bringing out the rich colour of the sands.

The author and Osama

After breakfast at the hotel, it is time for the long drive back through the Atlas Mountains to Marrakech and then the flight home. The drive gives me time to ponder on my journey through Morocco, and to try and sum it all up. Of the railway journey I had no idea what to expect, and the clean, fast, expanding and efficient system took me very much by surprise. The people were a constant throughout and whenever I reached out to them they were always welcoming and friendly. The food was always good, if a little exotic, and my favourite meal was beef tajine at a wayside restaurant just outside Moulay Idris.

The thing that struck me most about this fascinating and exotic country was that it is a land of extreme contrasts, with a mixture of ancient and modern, rich and poor, beautiful and barren, dry and lush – and all this is just three hours away.

King Mohammed VI has a plan for the future of Morocco called Vision 2010. This includes huge new tourist resorts along most of the Atlantic coastline, together with extensions and improvements to the road, rail and airport networks. Along with that will be all the trappings of mass tourism such as new hotels, golf courses, marinas, restaurants and bars and shops. The King's vision is that Morocco can create a tourist destination to rival all its competitors, with the hope of tripling their current three million visitors a year to something like ten million by 2010. Morocco has high unemployment, so this project will not only create huge numbers of much-needed new jobs but will also make a significant impact on the economic growth of the country.

I saw a lot of this development in Marrakech, but the sense of tradition and mediaeval living here is still very strong and, in what is an Islamic society, totally unlike ours. Despite all the new hotels that are going up it still only takes a short taxi ride to exchange the modern for the ancient.

When you are in the heart of the souk in old Fez, time seems to have no meaning. You are seeing, feeling, hearing and touching something that has basically not changed in a thousand years, and I cannot believe that an extra influx of tourists into Morocco will have a significant impact on that.

PART III

Russia 2010

The Trans Siberian Railway. The very words stir the imagination or, at the least, a desire to know more about it, or in my case when I can travel on it. So here I am in the early hours of the morning at Heathrow Terminal 5, sharing the arrivals area with about five other passengers who are all lying about in various stages of stupor. Fortunately, the Costa coffee shop is open all night and they have comfortable sofas.

The flight to Moscow is uneventful and we arrive at a very busy Domodedovo airport on a brilliantly bright and hot afternoon. The sun sparkles on the long sausage-shaped glass and steel airport building and in front of me stretches a wide tree-lined boulevard that leads to Moscow city centre some thirty miles away – but not today, as I will be flying on to Irkutsk later this evening so as to make the railway journey from east to west.

Domodedovo airport

Wandering down to end of the airport building I find the terminus of the fast and frequent electric train service between the airport and the city. There are two platforms and as one train glides silently in the other departs. There is an almost constant stream of passengers. I would very much like a photo of one of the trains but being conscious of the country that I am in and the possible sensitivity of taking pictures, it does not occur to me to try and take one without asking. It would be a shame to have my camera confiscated on the first day, or even to be locked up! There is an official on the gate but he speaks no English at all and shakes his head at my obvious requests to take a picture. After much cajoling and persuasion he agrees but makes it very clear that he wants me to do it quickly. Bureaucracy does not rule after all.

My luggage is checked in and I sit in one of the many coffee shops watching the world go past while I wait for my flight to be called: departure time 21.45, arrival time 07.45! A vision in leopardskin walks

Fast service to Moscow

past: trousers, jacket, bag and shoes all matching, she is hanging on the arm of a very soberly dressed man in a dark suit.

Eventually the flight is called and we take off at 21.30, followed by my first encounter with the time differences here, as when I next look at my watch it is ten past two on a dazzlingly beautiful morning. Irkutsk time is eight hours ahead of the UK and I am already starting to get a bit confused with the differences, although I do know that as we glide effortlessly and silently down through the clouds to a mist-shrouded Sunday morning at Irkutsk, it is still Saturday night in the UK.

Again, the airport is busy and they are very strict about collecting your luggage. If you do not have a bar code label stuck on your boarding pass that matches the one on your case, then you will not be reunited. Within ten minutes the scene outside the building is one of tranquillity; the street in front of me reminds me a bit of South America where in some towns the buildings and streets are festooned in electrical cables.

A coach is taking us to a local café for breakfast; the coach is a

Irkutsk airport

delightful period affair with plastic seating and colourful frilly curtains around the windows; there is even a frilled edging along the luggage rack. The driver is called Sergio but he is a man of very few words.

The journey is through what is obviously a poor part of the city; there are a lot of the old traditional nineteenth-century wooden houses with their ornate shutters and carvings but for the most part they seem neglected. I have also missed my first tram, as I was looking out of the other window.

Irkutsk tram lines

The view changes and there are some lovely old stone buildings side by side with some of the grey and forbidding office and tenement buildings of the Soviet era. They mostly have an uncared-for look. There are several dusty-looking parks with lots of trees but no colourful plants. I find out why later: those sorts of plants come so much later here because it is Siberia, temperatures here can be as low as minus 50 degrees centigrade in the winter and they have quite short summers. On this beautiful warm and sunny morning it is difficult to imagine that this place might be 50 degrees below freezing in a few months' time.

Breakfast is in a delightful little café under the 18,000-seater sports stadium of the city and starts with salami, cheese and almonds followed by sweet and salty porridge (it was very nice). Next is fried egg with cucumber, peas and a frankfurter with as much fresh bread and coffee as you want. But today is not about Irkutsk, as I will be here again in two or three days' time.

The coach now takes us on the 40-odd mile journey to Listvyanka on the shores of Lake Baikal, where I will spend one night at the hotel Myak before taking a boat trip across the lake to Port Baikal for the start of my railway journey. Once we clear Irkutsk the view is almost unchanging, with picturesque taiga forest on each side of the road as we drive up and down hills; the majority of the trees seem to be silver birch. It is very hot today and the air conditioning in this old coach is welcome. It seems strange to reflect that in the winter the temperature in Irkutsk can be so low, although it is also a dry area with little wind and the locals say that because of that the cold is quite bearable. I have read about Lake Baikal and have wanted to visit it for a long time, so the opportunity to combine a visit to the lake with a journey on the Trans Siberian Railway was very much a 'must-do'.

The first sight of Lake Baikal does not disappoint. As we round a bend in the road I catch my first glimpse of its shimmering surface through the gently waving branches of silver birch trees. The lake is blue, the sky is blue, the sun is bright and already I start to feel the magic of this place.

A glimpse of Baikal

Lake Baikal, or as it is also known The Pearl of Siberia, is a majestic expanse of water in an area of outstanding beauty, with evergreen forested shores and a backdrop of mountains that seem to march on for ever. Beyond the forested slopes are the snow topped Barguzin mountains. In the summer its blue waters are crystal clear to a depth of over 100 feet. The lake is in a rift valley and its age is estimated at about 25 million years; it is the deepest lake in the world and contains 20% of the world's fresh water. Below the lake there are some four miles of sediment, and core analysis from this has given climatic data from the last 250,000 years. The lake is nearly four hundred miles long and over a mile deep in the middle, and is so big that if all the rivers of the world flowed into it, it would take an entire year to fill it. Another interesting fact about the size of the lake is that all the rivers and streams that do now flow into it would take four hundred years to fill it. There is just one outflow and that is the Angara River on which Listvyanka is situated.

The lake region has a huge variety of animals and plants, many of which are found nowhere else in the world. Two of these are the nerpa, the world's only freshwater seal, and the omul salmon, very much a delicacy here. There are plenty of bears (more of those later), lynx, deer and sables, which thrive near the shore and in the richly forested mountains. Fish abound in the lake, including the famous sturgeon, and fishing is an industry here even when the lake is frozen in winter when some intrepid souls go onto the lake with tents and fish through holes in the ice that they have made. The lake has been commemorated several times with stamp issues including one in 1966 with several species of fish.

Baikal stamps, issued in 1966:
2K grayling, 4K sturgeon, 6K map of Baikal, 10K cisco, 12K whitefish

The minerals in the lake make the water so pure that it can be drunk without treatment; it's true, I tested it and although it was bitterly cold and I felt it all the way down my stomach, it had a clean fresh taste like nothing that I have ever had out of a tap.

Listvyanka is a fairly small town with a population of about 2500. It is situated at the south-west end of Lake Baikal and stretches eastward for nearly five miles from the mouth of the Angara river. The town is actually split into five parts with each one wedged into a cleft in the mountains. Listvyanka itself was founded in about 1650 by Russian pioneers who created a trading post here.

I am staying in the part of the town where most of the boats are moored and the marketstall people ply their trade. There is also a small shingle beach, which is very popular with Russian tourists. Some of the boats are of a considerable size, and looking out at the vast expanse of water in front of me it is very difficult to remember that it is actually a lake and not an ocean.

My hotel is the Hotel Myak, which in Russian means lighthouse and there are indeed similarities. The staff are very pleasant and helpful but speak virtually no English and it is time for me to expand my very limited Russian vocabulary from *da* and *niet.* I very quickly learn please, thank you, and my name is...

The Hotel Myak

First thing to see today is the Limnological Institute, or Museum of Baikal as it is also known. It is a modern, clean and cool building nestling within some spreading trees. On each side of the path there is a souvenir stall and one of the ladies is quite persistent, although not successful as I don't feel the need to buy t-shirts or Russian dolls, beautiful though they may be. The museum collects and displays information and exhibits about the origin and wildlife of the lake. There are samples of rock and minerals, several stuffed birds, and a particularly large and ferocious-looking fish with two rows of needle-sharp teeth. There are rows of bottles with preserved fish in them and other bottles the contents of which might be anything (unfortunately all the wording is in Russian) but look quite revolting, although they might well be of

Stuffed eagle with fish

historical significance. In the corner is a stuffed eagle with a fish in its grasp.

Next stop is lunch with a local family at their dacha (country house). It is very traditional and is built entirely of wood. The husband and wife, Tatiana and Sergei, are very welcoming and they are both keen cooks, as is their son Dennis. Most of these wooden houses are heated by wood burning and the favoured tree for that is the larch because it gives a good heat with very little ash.

Tatiana and Sergei's dacha

The dacha yard and the family hound

Lunch starts with two glasses of very strong vodka followed by a dish of mixed salad which is predominately chopped cabbage. This is followed by red cabbage and potato soup followed by mashed potatoes with meat balls. To finish there are some very nice home-made sweet biscuits, some delicate pastries filled with blueberries and apricots, and yet more vodka. They also make their own honey, which is quite delightful. The whole meal is both filling and delicious. Before I arrived in Russia I thought I did not like vodka, but it seems I was wrong.

Heading back to Listvyanka there is a stop for a chairlift ride to the

Tree carvings next door

In and around the village of Bolshaya Retshka

top of a mountain, to see spectacular views of the lake. As we rise slowly from the forest of silver birch, fir and larch I can see that the valley is being developed: there is a ski slope as well, which is open from December to March but not January as it is too cold then.

The ride has been well worth it and the view is indeed spectacular: below me is the start of the Angara river as it leaves the lake on its journey to Irkutsk. Through the heat haze I can see Port Baikal jutting out from the headland opposite; that is where the railway journey will start tomorrow afternoon as it follows the shore of the lake all the way to join the main line of the Trans Siberian at Slyudyanka some 50 miles away.

The chairlift

I opt to walk back down, as the track that meanders down through the trees is very enticing; the heat of the sun is mellowed by the trees and the only sound is of birds chattering. It is incredibly peaceful and this translates itself to me. It is a fairly long walk but without seeming to, I have come a great way and can already see the chairlift station in the distance and the girl with the ice cream stand and its melted contents.

Port Baikal

I bought a choc ice on the way up and it poured onto my hand as I opened it. My mind is obviously elsewhere, for as I pass some trees on a bend near the bottom I come face to face with a brown bear.

It is about 20 feet away. I stand in a state of indecision. Its lack of movement gives me confidence to pass, giving it a wide berth, but when I look back it still has not moved. It dawns on me that it might not be real, and with a feeling of stupidity and relief I cross to inspect it. It is extremely lifelike with real fur and unwinking eyes, and may well have been a real bear at some time. It has obviously been put here for authenticity and to give people like me a bit of a fright. It might seem a bit stupid to be taken in by it, but I already had it in mind that bears roam freely in these forests and so it was probably natural to assume it was real.

There will be more of Listvyanka tomorrow but for now it is time to return to the Hotel Myak for my first night in a bed since Thursday – it is now Sunday! There is plenty of time for a shower and change of clothes before dinner, which is chopped pasta and cabbage mixture followed by the local fish with rice and salad, and cake with cream to finish. It is not the type of meal that I am used to for dinner, but it was very nice and I certainly did not want anything else afterwards.

Time for a stroll along the waterfront where most of the stall holders that were here this morning have now gone. It is very much a time to stop and reflect where I actually am, for there can always be a danger that you visit a place and then leave it without really appreciating why you came here in the first place.

For me the reason for coming is easy: I wanted to travel on the Trans Siberian Railway, but in equal measure I also wanted to visit Lake Baikal. The statistics and location of this lake coupled with its uniqueness make it very special. There was another reason as well and that was to include the Circum-Baikal Railway on my journey, as this stretch of track is very rarely part of any other Trans Siberian Railway journey. Its mammoth construction with its many tunnels, bridges and walls, together with its beautiful location alongside the lake for all of its length, are bound to make it a visual treat.

As I sit here and watch the water gently lap the shingle beach and see the clouds slowly gather as night draws near, I reflect that I am in Siberia and a long way from home. It makes me realise that I am fortunate to be able to visit this and other interesting and beautiful places around the world.

Sunset over Lake Baikal

Monday morning and eggs, porridge and fruit for breakfast. Last night was a bit disturbed as I was woken by a knocking on the door at 11.30 pm; it was a maintenance man saying that there was sound of running water in the hotel and could he check my bathroom. It was apparently elsewhere, as he found nothing amiss. I have written this as though we had a conversation, but he spoke no English at all and it was all done with gestures.

Time for a gentle stroll along this part of Listvyanka to see if I can find some souvenir postcards. It is already quite hot. There is a fascinating variety of buildings here with a small tenement block in the middle of some traditional old wooden houses and a lovely little blue painted wooden building that is the local school. The school has a nice grassy playground and the whole place nestles serenely under some larch trees. Just off the main road there is a seal aquarium, housed in a long sausage-shaped aluminium building, but it is closed today. The long dusty high street is very quiet and there is little traffic. The local post office is only able to supply me with three postcards but further down the road I find a small shop selling all sorts of things, including some lovely packs of cards of Baikal and the surrounding area.

In and around Listvyanka

At the end of the street there is a small market and here you can buy the local fish in almost any form you want; I can see smoked, dried and fresh. There is a little dog sitting hopefully by one of the stalls or maybe he is just keeping out of the sun. There are stalls selling souvenir goods such as Russian dolls, Baikal stones and all sorts of jewellery but they seem very expensive to me. One stall is also selling soft toys and there is a delightful little white nerpa just waiting for me to buy it. The girl on the stall is called Alexandria and she has been working on

Alexandria and the hopeful doggy

this stall since she left school; she has virtually no English but it is quite easy to conduct a sale. She is happy to accept US dollars which surprises me as I had been told that you would only be able to pay for things in roubles.

I return to the water's edge and wait for the boat that will take us for a cruise on the lake before depositing us at Port Baikal where the train will be waiting. Looking out across this vast expanse of water it is more like looking at an ocean than a lake. Although it is calm today the lake does have its moods, particularly in the autumn when there are more than 15 stormy days a month. There are also several different winds that blow on this lake, all with their own name.

Verkhovik blows in the autumn from the north when the weather is bright, but when the wind gets stronger Baikal turns black with large waves on the southern shore of the lake. Kultuk also blows from the north but everything is grey and dull and the waves can reach 10 feet high. The most dangerous winds are the gornaya and the sarma, both of which come from the north-west; the sarma can reach hurricane force.

Waiting for the boat

Between Listvyanka and Port Baikal, where you join the Circum-Baikal Railway, there is a regular and well-used ferry service. From Port Baikal the line hugs the shore for the 56 miles that it covers on the trip eastwards through the Pribaikalski National Park to Slyudyanka at the extreme southern end of the lake, where it joins the main Trans Siberian line from Moscow to Bejing via Ulan Ude in Mongolia.

The original Trans Siberian railway ran along the Angara River from Irkutsk to Port Baikal on the west shore and was completed in 1900. At the same time on the east side of the lake a railway had been completed from Sretensk to Mysovaya (now the town of Babushkin, named after Ivan Babushkin who was arrested and executed at Mysovaya

Station in 1906). In order to establish a through railway connection the Russian government ordered a ferry/ice breaker from Newcastle, UK, to link the shores of the lake by transporting trains, cargo and passengers between the two termini. Sometimes in the winter they laid temporary rails across the ice although there were occasions when the ice broke under the weight of the train. The ferry was assembled in a specially built boatyard in Listvyanka and was named the *Baikal.* Three years later a further ferry was ordered, this one named the *Angara.*

The ice breaker and ferry *Baikal* leaving port in 1913

Meanwhile, the construction of the Circum-Baikal railway had continued and by the time it was finished four years had passed. With its 33 tunnels and 200 bridges it has become a lasting testament not only to the skill and courage of the Russian, Polish, Italian and English workers who constructed it, but also to the best of Russian engineering design. With the completion of the Circum-Baikal the link by rail was completed and a regular transport of goods and passengers began. The Circum-Baikal Railway was called the 'the golden buckle on the steel belt of Russia'.

Leaving Listvyanka

A spotless blue and white boat arrives and it is not long before we are under way on a beautiful day with the sun glinting on the clear blue water and a fresh breeze ruffling through my hair. The boat makes a sweeping curve and then follows the coast as the town of Listvyanka falls astern.

On a forest-covered mountain there is what looks like a white tower, which I later find out is the Baikal Astrophysical Observatory, the main purpose of which is to measure solar magnetic fields. It is perched on the top of the mountain, among the forest, at over 6500 feet above sea level and towers above what looks like a new hotel under construction.

Baikal Astrophysical Observatory

This sleepy-looking town is therefore not only up with the twenty-first century but is also the birthplace of a famous modern Russian, also connected with space. He is Alexie Leonov and was the first man to walk in space when he floated outside Voskhod 2 for 12 minutes in March 1965. He has been awarded the 'Hero of the Soviet Union' twice, and the 'Order of Lenin', and has also been commemorated on several postage stamp issues.

A block of 1968 Russian postage stamps genuinely autographed by Leonov

From the water we can better appreciate the majesty of the mountains, which rise and fall as they surround the lake. On the other side of the boat is water as far as the eye can see. It feels good to be part, if only for a short time, of this Russian boat with its Russian crew on this Russian lake. About 45 minutes later we approach Port Baikal and I can see the train parked near the water's edge.

First glimpse of the train

A long jetty stretches out, with the harbour behind it where there are some very modern and expensive-looking boats moored. The jetty here is edged with timbers that have definitely seen better days and instead of heading for the harbour, the boat skipper demonstrates his own way of landing by ramming the bow of the boat up against these timbers and then dropping a gang plank on them.

All ashore

Port Baikal is interesting and also a place of great contrasts. The port itself has a definite run-down air with decaying timbers, broken concrete and rusting hulks of unwanted ships, but new and expensive boats still use this place. Parked on a stretch of line by the water's edge is a steam locomotive of 1940s vintage, complete with red Russian star on the boiler door. Despite the general air of neglect it is still quite easy to see that this place was once a very important part of the Trans Siberian Railway, and this was recognised in 2005 when the station building was reconstructed, complete with an exhibition devoted to the Circum-Baikal. At the other end of the Circum-Baikal, Slyudyanka station was also rebuilt.

In and around Port Baikal

Ours is a long train of about 20 carriages in different colours with yellow/red, grey and others in shades of blue. I meet Tatiana and Natasha who are the attendants for the carriage that my berth is in, and after some negotiation I manage to get a four-berth compartment to myself. It is very comfortable and I spread myself out and wait, with great anticipation, for the start of this long journey.

At 3.20 pm we are under way and almost straight away there is a

Travelling from Port Baikal to Ulanovu

visual feast outside. I have the opportunity to ride on the locomotive and this is not to be missed. The line twists and turns as it follows every curve of the coastline between the mountains and the lake, and the views are stunning; there are many tunnels and the brightness of the sun almost hurts as you emerge from each one. Looking back, the mountains behind Listvyanka in the distance form a lovely backdrop to the long rake of colourful carriages as the train wends its way alongside this beautiful, clean and achingly blue lake. There is a boat slowly crossing the lake nearby and for a while it is almost a race as the train is going at a very slow pace – we just about win. Despite the heat there are still occasional ice floes at the edge of the lake.

Travelling along this line today as it follows the curves of the lake through some very remote country, mostly without roads, it is difficult to comprehend that all the materials for this mammoth construction were brought here either by barge or, when the lake was frozen, by animal-drawn carts. In 1949 an alternative rail route from Irkutsk to Slyudyanka was constructed that avoided the Angara river and Baikal, and as this new route considerably shortened the distance compared with the Circum-Baikal, traffic was transferred to this line. A year later work was started on the Irkutsk hydroelectric plant and in 1956 some of the railway from Irkutsk to Port Baikal was flooded as part of a new reservoir following the construction of a dam.

Circum-Baikal Railway view from 1910 showing double track

The construction of the dam effectively meant that the Circum-Baikal Railway became a 'dead end' and there was a dramatic drop in traffic on it. Because of this the line was reduced from double track to single track, although travelling along it today there is still plenty of evidence of its greater importance with bridges and tunnels now without lines. Currently, just a locomotive and two cars once a day transfer necessities such as vodka, salt and bread to the local inhabitants along the line. We stop at Ulanovo to let this train pass, but the stop is also an opportunity for the passengers to enjoy the scenery and have a walk alongside the lake as we will be here for about an hour.

Ulanovu

Ulanovu is a pleasant place and the train has stopped near some trees; the shade is welcome as it is quite hot and there are some mosquitoes about. There are some wooden houses used by residents and visitors and a pleasant little walk brings me to a jetty on the edge of the lake; there is an ice floe nudging against the timbers which is a bit remarkable considering that the temperature today is nearing 30°C. There are a lot of passengers on the train and a fair number of them are enjoying a leisurely walk along the beach. I join them to collect some of the brilliant white stones that are at the water's edge: dipping my fingers into the water I find again that it is still bitingly cold despite the hot weather. The local train that is currently here provides a year-round lifeline service to the residents, as there are no roads.

Back on the locomotive we leave Ulanovu. It is just before 6.00 pm and our next stop is at Polovinnaya about eight miles further on, where there will be an opportunity for hardy souls to take a dip in the lake and during the evening there will be a barbecue. The train is scheduled to leave Polovinnaya at 3.00 am – yes am. There are now more of the small ice floes about and not long after crossing one of the many bridges on this remarkable line we pass one or two very isolated wooden houses; it appears that the people who live in them depend on fishing and the supply train for their existence.

Isolated houses by the line to Polovinnaya

At nearly 7.00 pm we clear a half-mile tunnel and arrive at Polovinnaya, a small settlement nestling in a valley and surrounded by tree-covered mountains. There doesn't appear to be any way in or out of this place except on foot or by train. It is very picturesque here and is about the halfway spot on the Circum-Baikal. The population is mainly retired railway workers and as we arrive several women from the houses come out and welcome passengers into their home, a very old custom. Some of the staff of the train are busy setting up tables and getting things ready for the barbecue. I climb the hill that the tunnel passes under; inscribed on the arch of the tunnel is '1902–1904'. There are lovely views from here not only of the village itself but also of the train parked on a bridge and a small bay with a beach.

There is an old steam locomotive parked by the bridge and I stroll down to have a look and take some photographs. It is another 1940s vintage one and has been preserved on a small piece of track at the end of a brightly painted girder bridge. This bridge is the original and has been replaced with one made of concrete on which my trains stands; it spans a small tributary. The steam loco is remarkably clean and obviously well cared for, I guess by the retired railway workers but I forget to ask.

Polovinnaya

The barbecue is now under way and a man with an accordion has appeared; he has a good, if rather loud, voice and although I do not recognise anything that he sings, his audience are certainly with him. Tables have appeared, some with alcohol, some with soft drinks and several others that are laden with food which is roast pork, vegetables, onion, cucumber and thick brown bread; the food is very tasty indeed. Although you pay for the alcohol, the vodka is free! On another table are two samovars which are working hard in providing tea and coffee. There is a fire in the bottom of the samovar; you take the chimney off, poke sticks down the middle and hey presto, smoke and hot water.

I find the whole idea of a barbecue picnic by the side of the Trans Siberian

Map of the Circum-Baikal Railway
(courtesy of www.waytorussia.net travel guide)

Railway quite novel. There certainly cannot be many places where you can just leave a twenty-carriage train in the middle of nowhere for eight hours.

I head back to my compartment at about 9.00 to catch up on my notes, but the entertainment carries on for at least another two hours, until it starts to get dark. I'm not sure whether the mosquitoes have a hand in its ending but there are some of them about. Tatiana and Natasha are both in the carriage and Natasha makes me a cup of coffee before I settle down to my notes. At nearly midnight I finish writing but don't feel tired; my sleeping patterns seem to be a bit awry at the moment. At ten past three I am still awake and we start to move. There is a beautiful moon glistening on the water; yet another special memory of this part of the journey. We pass another station and out of habit I look at my watch: it is 3.40 am and the station is Maritui.

I must have dozed off because the next thing I know it is 6.00 am and we are stationary in Slyudyanka. This means that we have completed the Circum-Baikal Railway and are now on the main Trans Siberian rail route from Moscow to Bejing, via Ulan Ude in Mongolia.

Casting a rather bleary eye out of the window I see that we are actually in Slyudyanka station but on a siding, and I soon find out why. We are running a little late and this is an extremely busy station with marshalling yards and enormously long freight trains passing through every five minutes or so. We are kept out of the way in order not to disrupt this flow of obviously very important traffic which includes oil tankers, flatbed steel, agricultural machines, timber, box cars, bulldozers, containers, lorries and electrical generators.

We wait there a long time, a lot of it sitting in the dining car enjoying an early breakfast of cheese, ham, thick cut bread and butter, frankfurters, fresh orange juice and coffee, and people-watching the early risers on the platform. Eventually, the train departs on what is now a four-track

Slyudyanka station

mainline on a route that is completely electrified. I don't expect to pass any steam trains on the way as there have not been any on the Trans Siberian since 1987.

The journey to Irkutsk is mostly through thick taiga forest with occasional areas of devastation where the timber has been harvested and sometimes an old wooden house, almost in a clearing in the forest. It all seems very remote, although there is also the occasional larger settlement.

Kap station

We pass through several stations, all of them with marshalling yards and there is still an almost constant stream of freight traffic passing us. The Trans Siberian Railway is obviously an extremely busy and important part of Russia's transport network. Close to Irkutsk we pass a very clean and smart station called Kap, and as we reach the outskirts of Irkutsk the view is different from when I arrived at the airport, now of tall office and residential blocks mostly in grey but there is one bright orange one. As we pull into Irkutsk station 112 years after the first train arrived here I am impressed, for the station is a very attractive and nicely painted building with not a sign of litter or graffiti anywhere.

The town of Irkutsk was given city rights in 1686 and the first road between here and Moscow was built in 1760. This road led to a significant economic benefit for the town and area but perhaps more significant was the arrival of that first train of the Great Siberian Railway in 1898; from then on there was a greater influx of people to the area.

Outside Irkutsk station

Irkutsk is a reasonably compact city, particularly in its historic centre and is divided by the Angara river which is very wide at this point. The station backs onto the river on one side but it is only a short coach drive across the bridge to the Irkutsk Hotel on the other side, where I will spend one night before the next part of this journey to Novosibirsk. The hotel looks grey and dusty outside but inside is very smart with marble and nice plants dotted about. In the foyer there is a small exhibition of paintings by Yevgeny Ushakov; they are all of similar colour and style and appear to relate to the history of Irkutsk and the surrounding area. I cannot find out anything about the artist; perhaps he is just a local artist, but I find his pictures very interesting, particularly in the detail.

A painting by Yevgeny Ushakov: 'The Founder of Irkutsk'

The hotel is in an area of nice parks and buildings, close to the centre, and from my seventh-floor bedroom window I have a lovely view across the river to the railway station.

The view from my hotel

* * *

First thing the next morning is a visit to St Nicholas church by Lake Baikal. It was not possible to visit it yesterday but by coach it is a fairly short journey. The church nestles among the trees and is made entirely of wood; it was originally constructed in the nineteenth century by a Russian merchant called Ksenofont Serebryakov and the legend with it says that he was crossing Lake Baikal when a terrible storm blew up and fearing for his life, he prayed to St Nicholas, the protector of navigators. St Nicholas came to him and he was saved and the merchant then promised to build a temple in his honour. It was started at the source of the Angara river and finished in 1846 after the merchant's death, by his wife Natalya. In 1957 following the construction of a dam for the Irkutsk hydroelectric power station which caused the level of the lake to rise, the church was moved to its present location in Krestovsky Dell.

St Nicholas church

Inside there is an air of simplicity but there are also a lot elaborate icons and coloured tapestries, some from the eighteenth century. There are a lot of candles burning. Outside it is very peaceful with just the sound of birds. Round the corner I come upon a cat sitting in the sun: he has had what I can only describe as a drastic haircut. Although he still has his coat of fur round his head and his tail, he has been completely shorn in between.

We head back to Irkutsk, but first there is a visit to the Taltsy Museum of Wooden Architecture and Ethnography. This museum is considered a valuable piece of Russia's cultural heritage and was founded in 1969. It covers an area of about 165 acres and has many different wooden buildings on display. There is a pleasant walk to it through some trees from the car park but, once there and out of the trees, it is very hot. I am still trying to come to terms with heat and Siberia although I have learned already that Siberia, and particularly Irkutsk, is a place of temperature extremes with the record high being 37°C and the record low being –49°C.

Too tired to care

When the dam was constructed on the Angara river for the hydroelectric power station, the level of Lake Baikal rose by about a metre and there was a danger of many old and historic houses and buildings being lost. All these buildings were transported here and re-erected; there are over 40 of them with the majority of them being of seventeenth- and eighteenth-century origin. The most valuable of the monuments are the Saviour's Gate tower from Ilimsk (1667) and the Kazan chapel (1679). Other monuments include houses, barns, churches, offices, schools and a stockade.

It is a beautifully spread-out place with lots of grassed areas and convenient paths, and the monuments do not encroach on each other. There is a discreetly hidden café in one of the buildings and a police

The Taltsy Museum of Wooden Architecture and Ethnography

office in another; there are also some stalls selling souvenirs. Because it is so hot I take to moving from the shade of one building to the shade of the next. There are some steps down the side of a small house and underneath the building is a lovely cool cellar. There is a school, eerily empty as it never has pupils; on the wall of one of its rooms there is a picture of the Tsar. Nearby there is a farm building and inside it are a sled and a long four-wheeled cart for carrying barrels, together with several fearsome-looking implements.

Just behind the farm building the ground drops away and there is thick undergrowth and many lovely silver birch trees. Between the branches I can see the sun glinting on the water of Lake Baikal. I think this must be the edge of the museum site but the promise of coolness in the trees and the sight of the water lure me on; it is a good job that I'm wearing stout shoes. Where the ground falls away to the lake there is a very small wooden house among the trees with two shuttered windows and a locked door. Sitting on the doorstep listening to the sighing of the wind as it gently rustles the branches, and watching the ever-changing patterns of sunlight on the ground, I am quite at peace with this place. But it is soon time to move on, as there is a visit arranged to the house of one of the Decembrists in Irkutsk.

We make our way back through the taiga forest to Irkutsk to see the museum of one of the Decembrists. This particular one is situated behind the Transfiguration Church just off Timuryazeve Street and was once the exiled home of the Grand Duke Volkonsky. On 14 December 1825 Lieutenant Panov and other army officers marched troops into Senate Square in St Petersburg protesting against Nicholas I's assumption of the throne after his elder brother had abdicated. They also called for the abolition of serfdom and the introduction of democratic reforms. There was a long stand-off between the soldiers and troops loyal to the new tsar with occasional shooting. Eventually, the Tsar ordered cannon to fire on the protestors who were utterly routed.

On 3 January 1826 the protestors were finally defeated. The five leaders were arrested and put on trial in St Petersburg and sentenced to hang. As the hanging was taking place, the ropes parted before the five died, and according to an ancient tradition any prisoner who survived a hanging should have been set free. Nicholas refused to set them free, ordered new ropes, and they were hanged again. The five were Pavel Pestel, Kondraty Ryleyev, Sergey Muravyov-Apostol, Mikhail Bestuzhev-Ryumin and Pyotr Kakhovsky. Following the executions, most of the Decembrists (as they were called) were sent into brutal exile including Grand Duke Sergey Grigorievich Volkonsky. He had also been sentenced to death but this had been changed to 20 years' imprisonment with exile.

Volkonsky's house had originally been built in 1838 in the village of Uric, but in 1849 it was transported to Irkutsk where it stands today behind the Transfiguration Church. From the outside it is a fairly plain-looking building with a lot of windows, but it does also have an air of elegance. Volkonsky's house became the centre of Irkutsk culture and

Sergey Grigorievich Volkonsky, 1788–1865

social life: balls were organised, home plays were staged and popular musicians performed in the house. The Volkonskys lived there up to the amnesty of 1856, when it was sold to a merchant called Khaminov who organised a trade school for boys there. Meanwhile, Volkonsky returned to Moscow and again became an educated aristocrat.

After an eleven-year restoration the house was opened to the public in 1985 and today the interior reflects the Volkonsky's traditions and way of life, with the interior reconstructed with historical accuracy to complement the original furniture which has survived. The rooms are painted in bright colours and there are some nineteenth-century friezes. All the rooms are beautifully decorated and do indeed reflect another age. There is a grand salon upstairs and here we are treated to a classical concert with a male and female vocalist. They both have voices of some considerable power and although I was not able to follow much of what they were singing about, they were undoubtedly impressive. The grand piano in the room is the original one owned by the Volkonskys and is used several times today.

It is acknowledged that Volkonsky and all the other exiles made a great contribution to the history, geography, economy and ethnography of Siberia. The protest of the Decembrists has been commemorated in postage stamps, in 1950 for the 125th anniversary and again in 1975 for the 150th anniversary; both issues depicted portraits of the men who were executed.

A Decembrists commemorative stamp

It has been a busy day so far and as there are no more scheduled visits I return to the hotel. I intend to spend the rest of the afternoon exploring this historic part of the city.

Across from the hotel is a lovely tree-lined boulevard between the road and the Angara river and a short walk under the shade of the trees brings me to a statue of Alexander III on the embankment.

Alexander III

The view of the Irkitutsk railway station

Alexander (1845–1894) was born in St Petersburg and became Tsar of Russia when his father Alexander II was assassinated in 1881. As a young man, unlike his late father, he believed firmly in the dominance of the Russian autocracy and many of the reforms that he later brought about were to correct what he saw as the excessive liberal tendencies of his father. It was Alexander III who conceived the idea of the Grand Siberian Railway and it seems fitting that his statue here looks out across the Angara river to the splendid railway station on the other side which is part of his creation.

Nearby, there is another monument to a hero of Russia, Yuri Gagarin the first man in space, in April 1962. Immediately across the road is the start of Karl Marx Street and on the corner stands the Irkutsk Museum of Regional Studies. It is a very attractive building and its bricks and colours remind me a little of the White Star Line (owners of *Titanic*) building in Liverpool. It is built in the Mauritanian style with round windows and turrets.

The Irkutsk Museum of Regional Studies

The museum was founded in 1782 and is one of the oldest in Siberia; it has over 300,000 exhibits going back as far as Neolithic times, including minerals, weapons, tools, manuscripts (some from the seventeenth century), stuffed animals, clothing, handicrafts, ceremonial objects and ornaments. It also has the largest collection of coins in Siberia and a collection of jade objects from the New Stone Age. It is truly a place where you need to have at least a whole day to explore.

I walk past a very clean and functional-looking building. It is part of Irkutsk University, and a bit further on and across the road is the Drama Centre; this is a very impressive building with its columned front and green dome.

The Drama Theatre is undoubtedly an architectural gem and a credit

Irkutsk Drama Theatre

to Irkutsk. At night the columns and oval windows are highlighted by traditional lanterns on each side; the windows are also framed on the left and right by the dates 1894 and 1897. Looking at it today I find it hard to believe that this building was created in just three years by masons and carpenters who presumably worked mostly by hand. The grand opening of this theatre was on 30 August 1897, with prayers said in the foyer followed by celebrations in the main hall. The first production was held two days later on 2 September 1897 with a comedy by N.V. Gogol called 'Auditor'.

This part of the city has many attractive and interesting buildings and it is easy to get round it on foot. Turning at the top I find myself in Lenin Street, another historic name. There are tramlines in the street and sure enough here comes one right now. None of your fibreglass body and plastic windows with these trams, as apart from their more modern shape they look as though they were built many years ago and will probably last as long again. They may be providing a modern service but there is definitely a nostalgic air about them.

Looking up Lenin Street

There is a small café nearby and I ask for a coffee. The lady behind the counter has very little English and this leads to a certain amount of confusion when I ask for an Americano with cold milk. The rather predictable outcome of this pantomime is that she thinks I am an American and would like some milk. Still, I do get a coffee eventually, which is very strong but enjoyable.

I find my way to Sverdlov Street, which is a well-known name in Russian history as it was Yakov Sverdlov who directly ordered the killing of the Romanov family in Ykaterinburg in 1918. I come down here because I have seen a rather nice-looking church, and although it does not appear to be open it will make a good photograph if I can keep all the electricity wires out of shot. It is Michael Archangel Church and was originally constructed as a wooden building in 1738 and consecrated a year later to Kharlampiy the Martyr Archangel Michael. During a rather a chequered career it became a hostel in 1931, then it was the Irkutsk State University library, then it finally reverted to being a church again, and very nice it looks too.

Michael Archangel Church

I walk into a fairly large square and this, coupled with all the other things that I have seen and visited so far, convinces me that a combination of just Irkutsk and Lake Baikal would be a very nice holiday indeed. It does feel good, though, to relax on my hotel bed with a cup of coffee (not too strong), catch up on my notes and think about the train journey to Novosibirsk tomorrow. There are two great contrasts in my room: an extremely comfortable king-size bed and an extremely small bath. I have never seen such a small bath and I am sure that a person four feet tall would find it a bit cramped. I have to sit up straight to get my legs in, and getting my torso in the water means having my feet on the wall high above the taps. The water is nice and hot though and there is plenty of soap.

Irkutsk station is busy next morning and a large display shows all the trains that are leaving here in the next few hours. A big, red, sparkling clean TY2 locomotive, number 11973799, is ready to take me on the next part of this journey to Novosibirsk. The two attendants for the carriage that I am in, Natasha and Tatiana, are ready to greet their passengers as they come aboard, and are very kind to me with regular coffees and a smile.

Leaving Irkutsk

The long train eases out of the station and through marshalling yards and then through the suburbs of this very interesting town. The Angara river disappears from view and the lake that it comes from is already just a memory, but it is one that will stay with me for a long time.

I now regret my first impression of Irkutsk, as it has been a good and interesting place to visit with much to see and do, and complemented by Lake Baikal, just a forty-minute drive away.

We have been on the way for about an hour and the amount of freight traffic we have passed already has been phenomenal, with trains passing every ten minutes or so, mostly tankers.

We pass a large power station with a huge array of pipes marching across the countryside; it seems to go on for miles, then suddenly there is a substantial town. On the other side all the time has been forest.

On the train to Novosibirsk

At ten to twelve I ask one of the train staff what time we are due in Novosibirsk: the answer is 5.00 pm tomorrow. I am now starting to get some idea of the distances involved.

The view gives way to a wide grassy plain that stretches away to tree-covered mountains that are so far away that they appear to shimmer in the heat haze and are indistinct. I always had some sort of idea that the Trans Siberian Railway was a fairly busy passenger line running through some very remote and featureless terrain. I could not have been more wrong as the view is constantly changing and the line is obviously a very busy and important transport route for freight and passengers. This is the 'steel belt' to the 'golden buckle' that I mentioned earlier in connection with the Circum-Baikal Railway.

We arrive at a station called Zima, where there will be a locomotive change. I have learned that the locomotives only operate within a designated area and although I do not know whether the driver and his mate will be changed here, it seems likely. The view between Zima, which means 'winter', and Irkutsk has been one of forests, rivers, sweeping vistas, big marshalling yards and many settlements with traditional wooden houses, some very dilapidated, some very smart. I have also noticed that all the rivers that we have crossed have been in flood and in some cases the river has broken its banks.

Rivers in flood

Zima is a fairly small town but there has been a settlement here since the early eighteenth century and the area is low lying which might account for the flooded rivers that I have seen. The railway here intersects with the river Oka and although timber is important, most of the population either work on or depend on the railway. It is also the birthplace of Yevgeny Yevtushenko, poet, writer, film director, novelist and essayist. Through his works he was very critical of the Stalin period. In 1961 he wrote what became his best-known work, a poem entitled *Babi yar* about the Soviet distortion of the Nazi massacre of the Jewish population of Kiev, but the poem was also controversial as it spoke of the Soviet Union's persecution of the Jewish people.

Zima station

The absence of passengers at Zima is because this station is a freight marshalling and locomotive changing point only. I have been sitting in my compartment reading a Trans Siberian handbook, and I must have been engrossed because I almost miss Tulun, which we pass through without stopping. It is another railway town but it does have a passenger service. It is about ninety miles from Zima. In travelling round the world by train I have become used to seeing old steam locomotives preserved on a stretch of track near the station, but here in Tulun there is what appears to be a fairly modern electric locomotive in retirement.

Tulun station

We pass through an area of dense forest again and everywhere there is evidence of fires; the tallest of the trees have lush green tops but their trunks are burnt and blackened. It seems that these fires are just allowed to burn themselves out, but there are places where nature has asserted itself and the scorched ground is being covered with fresh grass and ferns.

Sitting in my compartment watching the ever-changing view of Siberia gliding past the windows, is both relaxing and interesting as stations come and go. There is Nizhneudinsk and several sawmills, so this is obviously logging country, and between here and Kamyshet the line twists its way through the Sayan mountains, a frontier between Russia and Mongolia.

We reach Tayshet and there is a short stop, but not at the platform so presumably we must be waiting for another train to clear the line ahead. I am disappointed as I wanted a photograph of Tayshet station, only because it is the junction for the Baikal Amur mainline, but my view is obscured on both sides by enormous rail tankers and box wagons. In railway terms this is a vast place.

After Tayshet and Bratsk the Baikal Amur mainline (BAM) runs about 400 miles north and parallel to the Trans Siberian Railway. The first section of the BAM to Bratsk was built in the 1930s with labour from the prisoners of the gulag system, and a lot of the eastern part was built during the Second World War also by gulag prisoners but supplemented by German and Japanese prisoners of war. In the days of Stalin there was prison camp at Tayshet.

The BAM was built as an alternative to the Trans Siberian Railway because of the possible vulnerability of that line near the Chinese border, and although work on it stopped for about twenty years after Stalin's death, interest was always there because of strained relations with China. Work began again in 1974 with the line eventually being declared completed in 1991. It is being considered as a container route between Europe and the Pacific, but as most of it is single track there are difficulties with that option.

The BAM is frequented by some western railway enthusiasts and it is possible I might yet become one of them, as this 2687-mile-long line not only skirts Lake Baikal at Nizheangarsk at the extreme north end of the lake some 420 miles from Tayshet, but also traverses what is almost unknown country to most westerners on its way to Sovetskaya Gavan on the Pacific coast.

After Tayshet the view again changes constantly as the train climbs and descends and crosses many rivers and ravines. I see at least two sawmills so this must be a big logging area as well. At just past 6 o'clock we go through Boshnyakovo: there does not seem to be anything of note to see here but just afterwards there is something unusual – a road alongside the railway. It is only a dirt road but is fairly busy with cars and a few lorries. There is a woman at the lineside feeding some large goats.

There are an amazing number of railway stations on this line, some of them with big marshalling yards and some of them only for railway workers. There are many settlements with traditional wooden houses, many of them quite poor-looking; virtually all of them have a cultivated patch of land with vegetables growing.

I am feeling hungry and abandon the window to head for the restaurant car which is eight coaches away. Dinner tonight is an interesting and very enjoyable meal with assorted fish followed by baked mushrooms with cream, cheese and a meat roll, followed by dessert. The meal is presided over by Alexander, resplendent in traditional costume.

Alexander

There is now a vodka tasting session, the drink that I have always professed not to like, but when in Russia… The first one seems slightly fiery but I am informed that I should drink it all at one go to get the best from it. I am not convinced by this explanation but am happy to go along with it. There are six different brands available and I discover that there is indeed a difference between them; previously I had always thought all vodka tasted the same. There is one that is pale brown in colour; this is from the production stage when they leave nuts (I think they said almonds) to soak in the vodka. It has a slightly mellow and very enjoyable taste. The evening progresses very satisfactorily and I am well into throwing the drinks back in one go. I am sure that I am not intoxicated, but on my eight-coach walk back to my compartment I think that I cannot put all the blame on the train for the swaying.

The nice dinner, the vodkas and the movement of the train all have the effect of making me sleepy, and stretched out on my bunk with a blanket over me and my head by the window I am soon asleep. This is unusual for me as I often don't sleep on a train, preferring to always see what is on the other side of the window, but the long journey and the several time zones have had their effect.

A new day with a bright blue sky and lots of fluffy clouds, and we arrive in Mariinsk. This was originally a village called Kiyskoye but it achieved town status in 1856 and one year later was renamed Mariinsk after the Empress Maria, wife of Tsar Alexander II. Gold was discovered here in the early part of the nineteenth century and for the next eighty-odd years the place was a boom town, but today the industry here is concentrated on tanneries and a soap works, and of course it is another important staging post for the railway, with marshalling yards and a locomotive repair depot. There is a twenty-minute stop here for another change of locomotive and this gives me an opportunity to get some bottled water from one of the little kiosks on the platform.

In and out of Mariinsk

We have swapped our red loco for a green one and it is a 1953 Skoda. It effortlessly pulls its twenty-coach train from the station and thereby must dispel some of the old jokes that abound about Skoda cars. The view changes quickly and we see a fire, though fortunately for us it has moved from the trackside.

Trackside fire in the forest

The line now curves away and it is all green again with many silver birch trees. There is a very swampy-looking field with what looks like an old army truck and even above the noise of our passing I can hear the driver revving his engine as he ploughs through the wet ground.

An old army truck negotiates the swamp

Stations come and go in the ever-changing kaleidoscope outside the window and we pass Tayga. The station here, at one time used to stand in the middle of dense taiga forest but now, from here, there is no forest as far as the eye can see. Tayga is another of those towns that owe their existence to the arrival of the Trans Siberian Railway and the station here was built in 1898. It is also the junction for a branch line to Tomsk, which is a very old city that was founded in 1604. When the Great Siberian Railway was being built it would have been a more appropriate route to go through Tomsk, as the town already sat on the great Siberian Post Road, but the town administrators did not want the railway as they feared it would break their trade monopolies, bring prices down and damage the local economy. When they eventually realised the railway would have exactly the opposite effect, it was too late to change the route.

Although not many westerners visit Tomsk it has plenty of interest with many old wooden houses, several universities, good shopping and eating, and also the KGB Memorial Museum which is in the former headquarters of that famous organisation. The visitors' book has Solzhenitsyn's signature in it. Novosibirsk is getting ever nearer and we pass Yurga, where there is an old steam locomotive on a plinth. There is also a lot of renewal work going on and new lines being constructed.

Yurga

A few miles further on and we slowly pass Bolotnaya, where there is an extremely attractive station. On a more mundane note I can also see a petrol station where, as far as I can tell, the cost of petrol is 55p per litre. Bolotnaya is a mere eighty miles from Novosibirsk.

Bolotnaya

We finally pull into Novosibirsk 27½ hours after leaving Irkutsk. Although Novosibirsk, which means 'New Siberia City', is Siberia's largest city and the third most populated after Moscow and St Petersburg, it did not exist until after the Trans Siberian Railway arrived. When it did, the city enjoyed considerable growth. The day that work was started on the railway bridge over the river Ob in 1893 is generally considered to be the day when the town was founded. The bridge was eventually completed in 1897. Novosibirsk is the geographical centre of Russia.

Inside and outside, the station building is very impressive and its glistening white is complemented by a pale shade of green. This glass-vaulted station, the largest in Siberia, took over ten years to build, which is easy to believe when you look at the quality of the building, especially the tower outside showing the time, the temperature and other information. There is a notice forbidding people to take photographs inside the station building, and that is a great pity as it is truly magnificent and you would think that they would be delighted for other people to know that. The entrance hall and waiting areas are spotlessly clean with gleaming marble floors; there are very large and exquisite chandeliers, and the high vaulted ceilings are adorned with intricate plasterwork. The waiting areas resemble very large ballrooms except that there is a profusion of large exotic plants in equally large containers, together with a fair number of leather sofas, truly a place where you would be only too pleased to have to wait.

Outside Novosibirsk station

Outside, a pleasant surprise awaits as there is a group of young women in national dress who welcome us with salt and bread in the traditional way, followed by a display of singing and dancing. I thought that perhaps a balalaika would be really traditional but a man with an accordion is very enthusiastic and the girls sing and dance quite delightfully.

We only have about two hours in Novosibirsk and will only be able to see the famous railway bridge, of which the town is very proud, and the opera house in Lenin square which is the town centre. We have hit this town at its rush hour and the coach is struggling to reach the park where the bridge starts; the journey is not helped by roadworks and the

Bread, salt and a musical greeting

local guide says that the town's road system has long been outgrown by the increase in the number of cars. We eventually make it to the tranquillity of the park and I am immediately struck by how wide the fast-flowing river is at this point. I can only wonder about the difficulties of constructing this bridge 117 years ago. The Ob is one of the longest rivers in the world and flows across Siberia for nearly two and a half thousand miles to Salekhard on the Gulf of Ob at the bottom of the Arctic Ocean. The people of Novosibirsk are so proud of their bridge that when the original was replaced in 1955 they kept a section of it and mounted it on a concrete plinth at the nearby water's edge. In the river there is an attractive fountain throwing its plumes of water towards the blue sky. Although this is pleasant spot to linger, time is pressing and we have to go.

The main square in Novosibirsk is Lenin Square on Krasny Prospekt and here is the magnificent opera house. It is architecturally beautiful and is the largest opera house in Russia; it also has its own ballet and

At the water's edge in Novosibirsk

opera companies. Today it has been transformed as there is a pop music festival outside and the noise is quite something. In a commanding position in front of the opera house is a grey-coloured statue of Lenin, together with three other statues of men in different dress but all holding a rifle; these statues are leftovers from the soviet era.

Lenin

It is time to go and as the coach leaves the square I catch a quick glimpse of the Chapel of St Nicholas. This small chapel was built in 1915 to symbolise the exact centre point of Russia and also to commemorate 300 years of Romanov rule. Today it sits incongruously in the middle of a dual carriageway.

I decide on an early night after an interesting dinner of salad with pickles, beans and eggs followed by thin slices of pork with vegetables and stewed fruit. Stretched out in my bunk, my last memory is of a great orange ball of a sunset.

Sometime during the night we pass through Omsk. I remember reading once that in terms of density there is more freight traffic between Novosibirsk and Omsk than on any other railway line in the world, and I didn't hear any of it! Despite the fact that Omsk is a very industrial city with large oil and gas fields, there are also many beautiful buildings there such as the Moscow Merchant Rows on Lenin Street, the Krestovozfvizhensky Cathedral and the Drama Theatre. It is only in the last twenty years that Omsk has been open to foreigners.

I have Russian porridge and pancakes for breakfast; the porridge is extremely sweet and a bit like rice pudding. I have made friends with Michael who is from Germany and it is nice to share experiences of other people and countries with him. We sit in the dining car drinking coffee and watching the world go past the window and it is very companionable, so the time goes quickly.

We pass through Tyumen. In railway terms this place is enormous with huge marshalling yards; travelling through a vast complex of lines at a speed that I estimate to be about thirty miles an hour, takes us nine minutes; it must be several times larger than Clapham Junction. Tyumen was founded in the sixteenth century and appears to have been growing at quite a rate ever since. Near the city hall there is a commemorative foundation stone to mark the centre of the city and the historic centre still has many old buildings. There are also lots of monuments to famous local people and the city is popular with tourists.

The weather has been quite wet for some time now and I have been relaxing and reading on my bunk and practising my Russian, but we are now only about ten miles from Ykaterinburg and the weather is brightening. Our first sight of Ykaterinburg is rows and rows of new cars lined up on a vast open space, presumably awaiting sale, and lots of electricity pylons; then we are into the station with its many lines. It has been 22 hours since we left Novosibirsk. Again, there is no overnight stop here and there will be just a few hours for me to see some of the centre of the city and a visit to the Church on the Blood. This modern and industrial city was founded by Peter the Great and today is the capital of the Ural region.

After the beauty of Novosibirsk railway station I had expected something similar here, but instead there are steep steps down from the platform into a long, damp and gloomy tunnel that leads to a spacious but ill-lit hall, with gold-plated chandeliers. The hall has a very religious theme with candles, icons, pictures of saints and a picture of Ipatiev House.

Outside the station it is packed with cars and taxis and despite the

Outside Ykaterinburg railway station

Nicholas 11
18/05/1868

Alexandra
06/06/1872

Olga
16/11/1895

Tatian
10/06/1897

Maria
26/01/1899

Anastasia
18/06/1901

Alexei
12/08/1904

The last House of Romanov

earlier rain the weather has now brightened up considerably. Ykaterinburg (or Sverdlovsk as it is still known by some people and also on some railway timetables) lies at the edge of the Urals. This mountain range stretches from the Kara Sea below the Arctic Ocean to Orenburg some 1500 miles south and is one of the oldest mountain ranges on the planet. It is also a rich mineral source for Russia; some of the minerals mined are beryl, platinum and quartz.

Ykaterinburg is perhaps most famous for being the place where the Romanov family were executed by the Bolsheviks in 1918. After Nicholas was compelled to abdicate, he and his family were taken to Tobolsk but later removed to Ykaterinburg. Towards the end of the First World War the red and white armies of Russia were engaged in a fierce civil war. The white Russians were pro the monarchy but were also, unwittingly, the probable cause of the death of the royal family, as they had surrounded Ykaterinburg. Because it looked as though the Tsar might be released, the Bolsheviks decided to kill them all and hide the remains.

The place where they met their end, on 17 July 1918, was in Ipatiev House, the property of a merchant by that name. The building was destroyed by the communist party in 1977 but in July 2003 the Cathedral on the Blood opened on the site of the former Ipatiev house and is today a much-visited place by both Russians and foreign tourists, now including myself. It is also a place where marrying couples come to have their photograph taken, and today there is almost a procession of them. All the brides are young and beautiful and some of the couples release white doves during their visit. Although I am obviously a tourist, one of the brides says thank you to me for taking her photograph. I have reproduced it here. Perhaps one day she will see it in my book.

Outside and all round the church there are very large posters of

Thank you

photographs of the Tsar and his family. Inside, the décor, pictures and fittings very much reflect that the Tsar was subsequently made a saint; upstairs there is a church within the church where a lone priest is conducting a mass under long drooping chandeliers, surrounded by tourists and visitors.

At the Church on the Blood

The Romanovs

I move on to the place that is considered to be the historical centre of the city. It is here that a dam was constructed, and although the dam is still here it has had a very wide and very busy road built over it. I stand in a beautifully paved courtyard taking a photograph; the water gushing from the dam passes under this courtyard and flows away on the other side with attractive flower borders and mown grass banks on either side. Nearby, there is a pretty little chapel that was built in 1995 in honour of St Catherine and the churches that the Soviets destroyed; it has a nice setting with a fountain and attractive trees for a backdrop but there is talk of demolishing it in order to build a large church here.

The dam

Across the road is very attractive building that to me looks a bit like a fancy decorated cake. It was once owned by a nineteenth-century merchant called Sevastyana, but is now a government building, and beautifully maintained.

The 'cake' house and the chapel

It is time to head back to the station but there is an opportunity to have a little wander around the station area first to soak up the atmosphere of this very busy place and watch the trams and brightly painted trolley buses go past. There is a very good tram system that gets you round the city quickly and at very little cost, and from what I have seen today with cars gridlocked in some places, the tram is the best option.

Walking back to the railway station I pass the old station, which is actually very close to the new one; it is a lovely building and it seems a shame that it is no longer used, although it appears to be well maintained. It was built in 1878 and use as a station was discontinued in 2003.

There is certainly plenty to see and do in Ykaterinburg, but for me, for now, it is time to get back aboard the train to relax and think about the next stop, which will be Kazan.

Around the railway station

After Ykaterinburg the train takes a different route from the perhaps more normal one of Perm and Novgorod, and between here and Kazan we pass some very old towns such as Krasnoufimsk, Sarapul, Agryz and Vjatskie Poljany. From Kazan our route then passes through Volga, Kanash, Sergatch Murom and finally into Moscow.

The old railway station at Ykaterinburg

There is a group of German tourists on the train and I am invited to join them all for dinner. They are very pleasant and good company and the time goes quickly. In future if anyone tells me that Germans do not have a sense of humour I shall dispute it, as I heard two very funny jokes which it would not be appropriate to repeat here except that one of them had something to do with a zebra and a pair of pyjamas.

Thanks to good food, good company and some vodka the evening is very successful and I head off to bed feeling relaxed although a bit tired, which I think is also partly to do with passing through all the time zones. At half past four I am woken up by the jolting of the train; we are moving slowly through a station that is again an obviously important railway centre with many lines and a locomotive repair depot. A little beyond the station we pass another of the old traditional wooden houses; it has a very neat front garden with lines of vegetables and even at this hour there is man busy hoeing weeds. I am not able to see a station name but I do see a kilometre post and from that I think it must have been Agryz.

We pass through a thickly forested area and as the long train follows a curve around the trees it reminds me of a lover's arm. Suddenly among the trees at the lineside there is a graveyard among the firs and silver birches; the gravestones and crosses are neatly spaced out between the trees and some of them are very colourfully decorated with flowers and ribbons. It seems as good as any and better than most as a final resting place which is obviously cared for.

The line passes through very lush countryside and there are lots of traditional wooden houses, sometimes just one or two of them and other times, small settlements. I see a fairly large town in the distance; it is built on a hill and between it and the railway there is a huge lake. The town's name is Arsk and it is situated on the banks of the Kazanka river

Between Ykaterinburg and Kazan

some 40 miles from Kazan. It is a very old town and was founded in the thirteenth century, but despite the fact that it has a population of about 20,000 it did not get town status until 2008.

Sixteen hours after we left Ykaterinburg we reach Kazan. Although it is still fairly early the sun is hot; today will be mostly a tour of the Kremlin and a boat trip on the Volga, before returning to the train in late afternoon. I am particularly looking forward to the boat trip as I have heard several versions of 'The Song of the Volga Boatmen' over the years, including a jazzy version by Glen Miller, and it will be good to be on a boat on that very famous river. The song is a traditional Russian one sung by the barge haulers of the river Volga.

The city of Kazan sits between the Volga and the Ural mountains and is also on the banks of the river Kazanka. Kazan Passazhirsky station is in the centre of the city and today it is big and busy with many trains. Outside it is the same, and somewhere in this melee of people, cars, taxis and coaches is a coach to take us to the Kremlin. The station was built in 1896 and today many intercity trains pass through for the eight million passengers who use it annually.

Kazan railway station

The first view of the Kremlin does not disappoint. At the end of a large forecourt is the dazzlingly white Spasskaya Tower, named after a local monastery. It is also the main entrance to this beautiful and ancient medieval town constructed on the site of a previous wooden fortress by Ivan the Terrible, using the famous builders in stone, Postnik Yakovlev and Ivan Shirjay. There is a lovely view from the courtyard and I see a pyramid-shaped structure that is a concert hall built in 2003. Just behind it is a soccer stadium and also an ice hockey stadium; when the latter was built the planners must not have thought a lot of their team as it is only a four-thousand-seater venue. Since then the local team have been Russian champions many times and the stadium has proved inadequate for the numbers attending matches.

Spasskaya Tower

The concert hall

Passing through the cool and lovely old stone-flagged entrance, the heat outside seems even more intense and I am glad to see a small stall selling water, among other things. Round the corner is Kremlin Street with a rather featureless building that houses the Military Cadet School and opposite that at the end of the street is the Kul-Sharif mosque. This gleaming white building has turquoise-topped towers at each corner and was only opened in 2005; part of the scheme for its restoration also included restoration of the sixteenth-century Annunciation Cathedral. This beautiful building is made from sandstone and has two lovely pale blue cupolas; it is also the oldest building inside the Kremlin.

There is a short walk through a shady courtyard and then back into the sun and on my left is the Soyembika Tower, generally regarded as

Annunciation Cathedral

Monument to the builders of Kazan

The Kul-Sharif mosque

The Soyembika Tower

seventeenth century and named after the last Queen of Kazan who, the legend says, threw herself from the topmost tier of the building after learning that Moscovite troops had captured the city. The tower is built in six layers and is 190 feet high.Who actually built the tower is not really known, although there are plenty of theories.

A man is driving a water bowser slowly along the cobbled path; it is emitting a very powerful jet of water from a nozzle at the front to clean the path, but the driver appears oblivious of the tourists that are about and some of them get quite wet.

Although largely reconstructed, the Kremlin still has its outer walls and towers, and from a high point near the President's Palace I can see a good example of the preserved walls. In the background I can see a very large and elaborate building and when I ask the local guide she says that it is the Ministry of Agriculture. After a last look across the Kazanka river towards the modern part of this nice city, it is time to head for the river port of Volga.

A short drive brings us to Volga River Port and it is quite a surprise. I suppose I had expected a fairly wide river with a few pleasure boats on it, but certainly not this huge expanse of water. The 'pleasure boats' look more like ocean-going liners and this is perhaps just as well, for

The Palace of the President

City walls

The Kazanka river

the calm and hot weather of this morning has vanished and in its place there are masses of forbidding cloud and a very stiff breeze that is whipping the waves up nicely.

The Volga is the longest river in Europe and rises in the Valdai Hills north of Moscow and then discharges some 2300 miles away in the Caspian Sea. It is the national river of Russia and is sometimes referred to as Mother Volga.

Mother Volga must be in a mood today for as soon as the boat leaves its mooring you can feel the effect of the waves. The shore falls astern as we head into the river proper and it becomes quite choppy. Most of the other passengers on the boat head for the indoor dining hall/saloon but I remember when I used to stand at the rail of a converted minesweeper fishing sixty miles out in the North Sea off Hartlepool, and although here there is no salt tang in the air the effect is much the same. I am really enjoying the wind tugging at my hair, and straddle my legs to match the movement of the boat as it punches its way through the waves. I wonder if the Volga boatmen would have gone out in this.

The Volga

The boat trip lasts about forty minutes and we pass a lonely little island covered in trees. Heading back into port we sail alongside a long peninsula with what looks like a derelict power station on it. For me it has been a very exhilarating experience.

There is still time for one more visit before the train leaves: we go to the Kazan State Conservatory. This architecturally elegant building is on a quiet street and is surrounded by other elegant and classical-style buildings. It was founded by Nazib Zhiganov, a famous Tatar composer, in 1945 and a plaque on the building outside proudly bears his name. It is one of the best higher-education institutions in Russia and in addition to young people from all over Russia, students from other parts of the world come here to study. The faculties include piano, orchestra, folk instruments, conducting, composition and Tatar musical art.

There is going to be a musical presentation by some of the young students of this conservatory and there are some 80 people gathered in a tastefully decorated hall with artistically draped curtains and a slightly raised stage on which are two grand pianos. The first presentation is a piano piece played by a ten-year-old girl. I do not catch the name of the work but she starts in a very loud and enthusiastic fashion, following up with a more contemplative piece before finishing with a flourish. The audience clearly enjoy it as much as I do, but there is a man nearby who quite clearly is neither listening nor interested in the music and I wonder why on earth he is here.

Next, there is a seven-year-old girl in a long blue dress and carrying a violin. She seems very assured for such a young person and treats us to what starts as a rather haunting little tune but then becomes quite jaunty. She is a first-year student here and as she finishes her playing, she is loudly applauded and there are cries of bravo. This charming little girl is followed by an eleven-year-old boy playing a piece by Chopin on the grand piano; although I do not know what it is called, it is delightful to listen to and the young man's fingers twinkle up and down the high notes.

We now see the return of the little girl who is accompanied on the piano by a ten-year-old girl in a flowing cream dress. I don't really enjoy this piece as there seems to be conflict between the piano and the violin, but that may be my lack of knowledge of the composition; they both certainly put their hearts into it.

They are followed by a young man of 15, very smartly dressed in black, who treats us to a piano concerto by Tchaikovsky. He gives the appearance of being in charge of his piano and confident that it will do what he wants it to do, and the result is, in my opinion, an inspired piece of playing. He is followed by an 18-year-old girl on the violin accompanied by a boy of 17 on the piano. I am thinking that the violin, piece is a bit on the mournful side until suddenly it comes alive as she makes the bow fly across the strings, producing an exciting and vibrant sound. They certainly have some extremely good young talent here as a girl of 16 demonstrates on the piano; the music she produces is urgent, stimulating, exciting, and we almost hold our breath listening to it.

Concert performers take a bow at the Kazan State Conservatory

After appreciative applause a 17-year-old blonde girl comes on stage and also gives an inspired performance, this time on the violin, especially when she produces what seem to be almost impossibly high notes. The piece is very familiar to me but my lack of knowledge prevents me from identifying it. She gets the longest applause yet. The last piece of music we hear is by George Gershwin and is performed on the piano by two brothers; it is played with style and quite clearly the audience enjoyed it.

The whole concert has lasted a little over an hour and has been a wonderful demonstration of the young musical talent that Russia has. I have an opportunity to speak with two of them afterwards and despite their obvious talent; they are modest and clearly love what they do.

Two young performers from the Conservatory

There is a very convivial mood on the train tonight as people enjoy what will be the last night on the Trans Siberian Railway before we reach Moscow tomorrow morning. After a meal of roast beef with Caucasian plum sauce followed by stuffed cabbage à la Babouschka with Madeira sauce, and then sweetmeats with coffee, it is time to relax. I join in the ebb and flow of conversation; it is not difficult to communicate and make friends even when language is a problem, especially when vodka flows freely. By the time I head back to my compartment seven or eight carriages away I am reasonably tired and ready for my bed, but must first catch up on my notes and pack ready for the transfer to the Renaissance Hotel tomorrow. Moscow is about 490 miles from Kazan so by the time daylight arrives we should be pretty close to the end of this rail journey.

After drifting off to sleep I am woken by a lack of movement. We have stopped somewhere, certainly not in any station, but I am glad to be awake as there is a lovely sunrise. I'm not sure of the time but it must be about 4.30 am and I lie in my bunk watching the sun slowly creeping up until it is a complete and dazzling globe.

Sunrise

Working out times I think we might be somewhere near Arzamas. This place has an interesting history as it was founded by Ivan the Terrible in the sixteenth century and in the eighteenth century was given city status by Catherine the Great – certainly great beginnings. There are also many churches but perhaps the loveliest of them is the Resurrection Cathedral built to celebrate Russia's victory over Napoleon in 1812. It has a very classical look with several columns.

Unfortunately, Arzamas is remembered for something tragic as well, for in June 1988 three wagons on a freight train blew up here. The wagons were carrying hexogen and the effects of the explosion were catastrophic with more than ninety people killed and one hundred and fifty injured, as well as considerable property damage. Hexogen is a powerful explosive developed during the Second World War and is usually mixed with waxes, in plastic explosives such as Semtex.

We are just about fifty miles from Moscow and for an hour the view

Approaching Moscow

on each side has been of continuous forest made up of silver birch and fir trees, with occasional rivers and green expanses. Between the trees and the train there are masses of purple and white lupins mixed with buttercups; it all looks very picturesque. The end of this exciting, interesting and highly enjoyable railway journey is now very near as we pass the tall apartment buildings and office blocks of the outskirts of Moscow.

Finally, the journey ends as we glide smoothly into Kazansky rail terminal and the quiet platform suddenly becomes thronged with people from this twenty-coach train. Inside, the terminal is bright, clean and airy and outside the façade is a lovely combination of russet and white; the building is acknowledged to be perhaps the most beautiful of all of Moscow's nine rail terminals. Outside, passengers who have just arrived have either melted away or been absorbed by the coaches and mini buses parked nearby; within ten minutes the forecourt of the station has resumed its former more peaceful self.

The station has two main lines, one serving the south-east and the other serving Kazan. It was built in 1864 and then later rebuilt during a period covering 1913 to 1940. It is situated on Komsomolskaya Square which is also home to two other rail terminals, Leningradsky and Yaroslavsky; on this square near Leningradsky rail terminal there is an interesting combination of beautiful classical buildings and the severe architecture of the Stalinist period.

The final locomotive of this long trip

* * *

There are four main options for travelling the Trans Siberian Railway and they are: (1) The Trans Manchurian from Moscow to Bejing, via Harbin in China; (2) The Trans Mongolian from Moscow to Bejing via

Outside Kazansky rail terminal

Ulan Bataar in Mongolia; (3) The Trans Siberian from Moscow to Vladivostok, entirely through Russia and considered by the purists to be *the* Trans Siberian rail journey. There is also (4) the Trans Siberian from Moscow to Tayshet and from there on the Baikal Amur mainline (BAM) to Sovetskaya Gavan on the Pacific coast; this is the most northerly of the routes and almost certainly the least used by western travellers.

The Trans Siberian railway to Vladivostok is the world's longest continuous railway at 5780 miles and, as mentioned earlier, the idea of it was conceived by Tsar Alexander III. Work started on its construction in 1891, and it was eventually completed in 1916 when the bridge at Khabarovsk, the last main stop before Vladivostok, was finished. As you travel along it today behind modern and powerful locomotives, it is hard to imagine the difficulties and hardship endured by the people who built this magnificent line and although several sections were later rebuilt it stands testament to them to this day, remembering also that it was built mostly without any form of machinery.

My journey has been slightly different to those listed above, in that I wanted to spend more time at Listvyanka and Lake Baikal rather than Bejing or Vladivostok, so I flew direct to Irkutsk and then by coach to

Listvyanka. I then crossed the lake to join a group on a chartered train travelling from Bejing to Moscow, at Port Baikal.

Although the rail journey is over, I am staying one night in Moscow, and today and tomorrow there will be an opportunity for me to visit the Kremlin and Red Square, not to mention the Metro.

First thing is lunch and this is at the Café Mockba in Brestskaya Street near Myakovskaya metro station. This station is beautifully decorated like most of the metro stations and is Art Deco styled inside. The café is on two floors and is all polished wood and subdued lighting; there is a nice atmosphere to it. The waitresses are very quick and efficient and I settle for what turns out to be a very nice and varied salad, which is enough for me after my rather large breakfast. The Café Mockba serves European as well as Russian cuisine and is open until midnight. It is a popular place for romantic dates.

Two views from the Café Mockba

Next stop is a visit to the Kremlin. I have been looking forward to this, especially after the visit to Kazan where I learned that the Kremlin is much more than a seat of government. The Moscow Kremlin is actually a v-shaped fortified and walled medieval town, with a history going back more than seven hundred years. It is now surrounded by trees on two sides and the Moskva river is on the far side from the entrance.

The security at the modern entrance building is very tight and my bag with cameras and batteries in it is scrutinised very carefully. From the entrance there is an inclined walkway to the Spasskaya Tower which is the entrance proper to the Kremlin; this inclined walkway actually used to be a bridge over a moat which was built to separate the Kremlin from the rest of the town but it was filled in the year after the defeat of Napoleon. From here, there is sight of the impressive Kremlin wall that was built in about 1490.

Outside and inside the Kremlin

The Kremlin is the official residence of the President of Russia and the palace that he uses for this function is very impressive. Everything, buildings, paths, roads, gardens, is spotlessly clean and tidy and there are a few policemen about whose role appears to be to keep the tourists tidy as well, by keeping them off the roads although there is no traffic.

The senate building, official residence of the President of Russia

Standing in what is called Cathedral Square on this very hot day, I am surrounded by beautiful cathedrals and palaces. The Cathedral of the Assumption is the oldest and largest, and dates from the fifteenth century although it does stand on the site of an earlier cathedral built in the early fourteenth century. The later building was commissioned by Ivan the Great in 1475, and he recruited Alberti Fioravanti from Italy to build him a symbol of the city's splendour. This work took Fioravanti about four years but when he requested to return to Italy after he had finished, Ivan imprisoned him and he died in prison a few years later.

Another beautiful cathedral just in front of me is the Cathedral of the Annunciation; this was used by the Tsars as their private chapel, and its many golden cupolas glisten in the bright sunlight.

The Cathedral of the Assumption

The Cathedral of the Annunciation

Nearby is the Cathedral of St Michael; this very Italian-style cathedral was the last of those commissioned by Ivan the Great. Strangely, the cupolas are in silver rather than the usual gold but it is none the less a very stylish building. The walls inside are lined with the coffins of members of the Russian royalty, including Ivan the Terrible.

The Cathedral of St Michael

The Tsar's Bell

On a concrete plinth by the Great Bell Tower is the Tsar's Bell. This huge bell is made of bronze and weighs 200 tons; it is about 20 feet high and is decorated with depictions of Tsar Alexei and his Empress Anna who commissioned the casting in 1735 from the pieces of an earlier bell. It was made by a local foundryman called Motorin, together with his son and about 200 other craftsmen, but while it was cooling off in its casting pit a fire began in the Kremlin and when water was thrown over the bell the large chunk that I can see in front of me broke off. It was left where it lay for nearly a hundred years until a local architect raised it and placed it where it is today. The bell tower itself dominates the Kremlin at over 250 feet and used to be the tallest structure in Russia.

Heading towards the exit via some welcome shade-giving trees I pass the Church of the Nativity with its colourful cupolas, and on my left there is a large incongruous and modern concrete building. It appears to be some sort of conference hall or meeting place, I am not sure which. Looking at all the beautiful buildings it is difficult to appreciate the extent of the destruction that has taken place here over the last four hundred years from demolition and replacement of original buildings to the effects of war. This place oozes history and it would be easy to research the Kremlin and extend this short description of my experience here into something approaching a book. I would only say to people thinking about visiting the Kremlin, read about its history first because it is truly fascinating and you will get the best from your visit.

Moscow from the Kremlin

The hotel for my short stay in this very interesting city is the Renaissance, which is in the cultural centre of Moscow and very close to the Kremlin, Red Square, the Bolshoi Theatre and the Pushkin Museum. It is next to the Olympijsky Exhibition Centre which was

The Renaissance Hotel

The view from my hotel bedroom window

originally built for the 1980 Olympic Games. The hotel is four-star and very comfortable, and I have a large and well-appointed room. Most of the staff seem to be fluent in English and German as well as Russian and they are very helpful. There is a very nice restaurant on the lower ground floor and the quality of the food and surroundings is very good.

After a fairly early dinner the plan for the evening is a ride on Moscow's famous metro and then a visit to Red Square. Construction of the metro started in the 1930s and the aim was to make them 'people's palaces', so famous artists and architects were employed in the design and construction. The result is that Moscow's rapid transit system has stations that are impressive, elegant and full of style, not to say architectural masterpieces.

Komsomolskaya station

Although it is now past rush hour the metro is still quite busy and it is not always easy to dawdle and look at the wonders of the stations when busy people are trying to get from A to B in the shortest time they can. The system currently carries about seven million people a day and serves most of the Moscow area through a series of radial lines from a central circular line. Trains run about every two minutes except late at night, but only until 1.00 am when the system shuts down for maintenance until about 5.30 am.

Although it is possible to get a map with the station names in English, a much better option is to try and master the Cyrillic alphabet, although that is no mean feat for a non-Russian.

Travelling on these trains is very like the metro systems of any other country: the difference is when you get off and find that the lighting is provided by chandeliers which cast their light on marble walls. There is no graffiti anywhere and everything is spotlessly clean. Most of the little tunnels that connect platforms have bronze figures on each side and the ones that I see are sports men and women, soldiers and farmers, although I am sure that there are other depictions as well.

More metro stations

When I leave the metro it is quite dark but the deep blue sky and floodlights on the buildings will, I feel sure, give me some nice photographs. Red Square: The name of the square seems to have originated in the seventeenth century from the Russian word 'Krasnaya' meaning red. I suppose for a lot of people the name conjures up images of military parades and armoured vehicles towing rockets, but although that is true the square has had a long and chequered history and has seen many changes. It has been a public market place and a place of public execution and public proclamations, and even the coronation place of some Tsars. In 1990 it was added to UNESCO's heritage list and about that time the military parades stopped, although they did recommence in 2008 with a sixty-third year anniversary parade celebrating the defeat of Nazi Germany.

During the Soviet era in 1936, and in order to allow access for heavy military vehicles to the square, the original early seventeenth-century

Red Square at night with the GUM building, St Basil's Cathedral and the Spasskaya Tower

Kazan Cathedral was demolished. It had been erected to mark the liberation of Moscow from Polish aggressors, by the Russian People's Volunteer Army in 1612. In 1990–1993 the Kazan Cathedral was reconstructed to the original design, using the measurements and drawings of the building that had been made before its destruction in 1936.

St Basil's Cathedral

Nowadays the square has many uses including pop concerts with famous performers such as Paul McCartney. It seems that I have arrived at a bad time, as a lot of the square is fenced off and they are obviously in the process of dismantling a vast amount of staging from some sort of event.

I have a memory of a light plane flying into Russian air space and, to the consternation and embarrassment of the Russian military, landing in Red Square. I had forgotten the date but on looking it up I find that it was in 1987, and that the pilot received a four-year prison sentence but was released as a goodwill gesture after about 12 months, following the agreement between Reagan and Gorbachev on nuclear weapons in Europe.

There is definitely a sense of history here, knowing that on this spot soldiers and the military might of Russia marched past successive soviet leaders, taking the salute. In front of the floodlit Kremlin wall is a granite cube-shaped building that is the Mausoleum of Vladimir Ilyich

Lenin; the embalmed body of the founder of Soviet Communism lies within. On the opposite side of the square is the GUM building (Glavnyi Universalnyi Magazin – translated as 'main department store'). It is a tall, three-storied, elegant and fashionable shopping mall built at the end of the nineteenth century. In 1917 the building had over a thousand stores inside, but today that figure is nearer two hundred and they are mostly designer shops and boutiques.

Lenin's mausoleum and the Kremlin wall

When the Bolsheviks came to power the GUM was nationalised and was a department store until 1928 when Stalin had it converted to offices. Following the death of Stalin the GUM was re-opened as a department store in 1957, and it later became privately owned by a big supermarket company following the end of the Soviet era. Tonight it is ablaze with lights and tomorrow morning I will have the opportunity to shop inside it.

Behind me is the State Historical Museum, a lovely dark-red brick building that was completed in the 1870s. It holds Russian history from

Glavnyi Universalnyi Magazin

Kievan Rus (about AD 880) to the present day and it looks very impressive with the floodlights nicely picking out the tall towers and pinnacles. It was opened by Tsar Alexander III.

State Historical Museum

It is time to head for the hotel and dinner, but tomorrow there will just be time to visit the GUM again, this time for shopping, before the 40-mile coach journey to the airport. The dinner is excellent and I opt for roast lamb with jacket potatoes and vegetables. It is such a substantial meal that I give dessert a miss, although I do manage a couple of vodkas afterwards. The king-size bed is quite a change after sleeping on the train so much, and I have a very good night's sleep.

Looking out of my bedroom window in the morning I can see that it is raining hard and has obviously been doing so for some time. Considering the blue skies and hot weather up to this point it is both surprising and disappointing; perhaps it is setting the mood because the journey has finished.

Red Square is wet this morning and it is nice to stroll inside the GUM for a bit. The architecture inside is splendid and it is a real pleasure to amble through the beautiful surroundings and cross from one level to another on the pretty little link bridges. I soon discover that it is indeed a very expensive place to shop, and the only bargain that I find is a bottle of vodka for about £8, although I could have Beluga vodka for £34 a bottle.

I look for a polo shirt with a Russian breast patch but the cheapest one that I find is £37 and I am not prepared to pay that for it. There are several shops selling chocolates and on their outside counters there are pyramids of all sorts of chocolates to tempt the unwary passer-by,

Inside the GUM building

from large white chocolate shells with gold swirls to ones that are mysteriously wrapped in gold or silver paper; there is no such thing as a vulgar price list on show.

Whatever the shop is selling, the item is always artistically displayed, in keeping with the surroundings I suppose; irrespective of the prices charged it is still a delightful place to wander round; there is even a pretty fountain with tinkling water and nearby seats to relax. Apart from two groups of tourists there are very few people around at the moment but it is a bit early.

Outside, Red Square looks a bit bedraggled after all the rain but still retains its fascination and I take some more photographs despite the rain, if only to contrast with last night's pictures.

Red Square and St Basil's Cathedral on a very wet morning

The coach appears on the car park behind St Basil's Cathedral. All that is left of my wonderful journey across Russia is about an hour's journey to the airport, although we will be passing some interesting landmarks on the way. The first one of these is the Bolshoi Theatre, a lovely classic-looking building where both ballet and opera are performed. As a ballet lover it is a real treat to be able to see, albeit briefly, the spiritual home of the Bolshoi Opera Company. The building I photograph was erected in 1824, and replaced an earlier one that had been destroyed by fire. I would imagine that the words 'Bolshoi Ballet' are known worldwide, even by non ballet lovers.

On the edge of an extremely busy street with cars apparently coming from all directions is the Ministry of Foreign Affairs. It is a skyscraper built in 1951 and although, in my opinion, it is very ugly, it is a wonderful example of the varied architecture that you find all over Russia. It is well over 500 feet high and was based on a similar building in New York.

On the banks of the Moskva river we have made a brief stop to look at the Cathedral of Christ the Saviour. When Napoleon retreated from Moscow in 1812, the then Tsar Alexander I decreed that a cathedral would be built in honour of Christ the Saviour for saving them from the peril that was upon them. There was a long delay caused by the death of Alexander and a change of sites and design. Work eventually started in 1839 but was not finished until 1860. The interior was very elaborate, with much use of marble and precious stones. In 1882 Tchaikovsky's 1812 overture was publicly played for the first time in this building.

After the death of Lenin, the Soviet regime decided to use the site to build a Palace of the Soviets and the cathedral was blown up in 1931. The new palace never materialised and in 1990 permission was given to rebuild the cathedral as an exact replica of the original. Work stated in 1994 and despite difficulties with design and construction the new building now stands before me in all its glory, and is a testament to the skill and commitment of those involved in replacing the original one.

The Bolshoi Theatre

Christ the Saviour Cathedral

And so at last to the airport. Inside, it is much like any other airport and as I walk through the door it is like turning the page of a book and finding that what has gone before is now just a memory. But that memory is crammed full with images of this multi-faceted nation and its long and turbulent history from which has come all the beautiful things that I have seen on this all-too-short journey. Perhaps there will be an opportunity for me to visit Russia again. I take with me, most of all, treasured memories of the new friendships I have made along the way.

Two new friends – Natasha and Tatiana